Lecture Notes in
Computer Science

Lecture Notes in Computer Science

Lecture Notes in Computer Science

Edited by G. Goos and J. Hartmanis

97

Shunji Osaki
Toshihiko Nishio

Reliability Evaluation of Some Fault-Tolerant Computer Architectures

Springer-Verlag
Berlin Heidelberg New York 1980

Authors

Shunji Osaki
Toshihiko Nishio
Dept. of Industrial Engineering
Faculty of Engineering
Hiroshima University
Hiroshima 730/Japan

AMS Subject Classifications (1980): 68 A 05
CR Subject Classifications (1974): 6.2, 6.3, 6.9

ISBN 3-540-10274-4 Springer-Verlag Berlin Heidelberg New York
ISBN 0-387-10274-4 Springer-Verlag New York Heidelberg Berlin

Printing and binding: Beltz Offsetdruck, Hemsbach/Bergstr.
2145/3140-543210

PREFACE

Computer systems play an important role in our society. A system
break-down is costly, dangerous, and even causes confusion in our society. It is, therefore, of great importance to build and operate such
systems with high degree of reliability. This book investigates stochastic models of some fault-tolerant computer architectures and ob-
tains the reliability and the performance-related reliability measures
by using a unique modification of regeneration point techniques in
Markov renewal processes. This book also gives numerical examples of
such reliability measures for comparisons of some fault-tolerant computer architectures from the viewpoints of the reliability and the
performance. Several interesting results are presented based on the
numerical examples. Such results are also of great use to design the
system configurations of the fault-tolerant computer architectures.
Throughout this book Markov renewal processes are applied to analyze
stochastic models. The Appendix is devoted to sketch briefly Markov
renewal processes.

The authors wish to thank M. Kajiyama and M. Kinugasa for their
helpful comments and suggestions. We are also grateful for the help
given by N. Kaio.

Shunji Osaki
Toshihiko Nishio

Hiroshima, JAPAN
April 1980

CONTENTS

CHAPTER 1

RELIABILITY MEASURES FOR COMPUTER SYSTEMS

1.1. Introduction

The remarkable progress of modern computer technology enables us to make large-scale computer systems which play an important role in our society. Examples of such systems are a vehicle traffic control system, a communication system, a banking system, a seat reservation system, and so on. A break-down of such a system may be costly, dangerous, and may cause confusion in our society. It is, therefore, of great importance to operate such a computer system with high reliability.

The concept of fault tolerance was introduced in the late 1960's on the above background, and the International Symposium on Fault-Tolerant Computing has been held every year since 1971. Avizienis (1976) defined a fault-tolerant system as follows: "It is a system which has the built-in capability (without external assistance) to preserve the continued correct execution of its programs and input/output functions in the presence of a certain set of operational faults. An operational fault is an unspecified (failure-induced) change in the value of one or more logic variables in the hardware of the system. It is the immediate consequence of a physical failure event. The event may be a permanent component failure, a temporary or intermittent component malfunction, or externally originating interference with the operation of the system. "Correct execution" means that the programs, the data, and the results do not contain errors, and the execution time does not exceed a specified limit. An error is the sympton of a fault, i.e., it is the change in an instruction or a data word which is caused by the presence of a fault at the point of the physical failure event."

Avizienis (1976) also defined a partially fault-tolerant ("fail-soft," "gracefully degrading") system as follows: "It is one which has the built-in capability to reduce its specified ("full") computing capacity and to "shrink" to a smaller system by discarding some previously used programs or by slowing down below the specified rate of execution. The reduction occurs because of decreases in the working hardware configuration that are due to operational faults. Another

cause of such "shrinking" may be the discovery of left-over design
faults in the hardware of programs."

In general, computer systems with high reliability can be achieved
by redundancy and/or maintenance techniques. The redundancy techniques
that have been developed to protect computer systems againist operational faults may assume three different forms; hardware (additional
components), software (special programs), and time (repetition of operations). See the details developed by Avizienis (1976) and Anderson
and Randell (1979). In this book, we discuss some computer architectures mainly from the viewpoint of the hardware redundancy. Throughout this book, the term "redundancy" has to be understood as "standby
redundancy" and not as "redundancy" for fault detection purposes, unless otherwise specified. The corrective maintenance techniques include
error detection, diagonosis, repair and/or replacement, and retry techniques. Another important maintenance techniques in computer systems
are the scheduled maintenance techniques which have been applied to
almost all computer systems to achieve high reliability and performance.
In this book, we discuss some repairable computer systems from the viewpoint of the corrective maintenance, where the repair is usually made
by replacing faulty components by new ones. We do not intend to discuss
the scheduled (or preventive) maintenance techniques in this book.

Beaudry (1978) proposed the following redundant computer systems
(computer systems with several processors (or units)) in four ways to
achieve high reliability:

(1) Massive Redundant System.
(2) Standby Redundant System.
(3) Hybrid Redundant System.
(4) Gracefully Degrading System.

The above redundant computer systems have their own characteristics of architectures, performance, and reliability as follows: (1)
Massive redundant systems, which use techniques such as triple-modular
redundancy (see von Neumann (1956)), N-modular redundancy (see Mathur
and Avizienis (1970)), self-purging redundancy (see Losq (1976)),
execute the same tasks on each equivalent unit and vote on the outputs
for improving the output information. A dual system, which is composed of two identical units, executes the same tasks on each identical
unit and checks the outputs. A dual system is one of the simplest massive redundant systems, and will be discussed in the later chapters.
(2) Standby redundant systems execute tasks on their active units.
Upon detection of the failure of an active unit, these systems attempt
to replace the faulty unit with a spare unit (see Bouricius et al.

(1969)). A <u>duplex system</u>, which is one of the simplest standby redundant systems, is composed of an active unit and a spare unit. A repairable duplex system will be discussed in the later chapters. (3) Hybrid redundant systems are composed of a massive redundant core with spares to replace failed units (see Losq (1976)). In Chapter 5, we shall discuss a hybrid redundant system with three units, which is composed of a two-unit gracefully degrading system (see below) and a standby unit. (4) Gracefully degrading systems may use all units to execute tasks, i.e., all failure-free units are active. When a unit failure is detected, these systems attempt to reconfigure to a system with one fewer units (see Borgerson and Freitas (1975)). A <u>multi</u> (multiple, multi-processor, multiple-processor) <u>system</u> is one of such gracefully degrading systems. In the later chapters, we shall discuss a multi system with two units (two processors and two storages). Mathur and de Souza (1975) proposed a general modular redundant system which includes the above four models as special cases.

In this chapter we discuss a simple N unit redundant (unrepairable or repairable) system from the viewpoint of the performance-related reliability measures. Beaudry (1978) proposed such performance-related reliability measures and discussed some simple mathematical models based on Markov processes. In this chapter, we discuss much more complicated models based on generalized assumptions. In the later chapters we shall discuss some redundant computer architectures based on Markov renewal processes and the corresponding reliability measures. Throughout this book we assume that the controllers are error-free, the modules are independent concerning errors, and errors are correctly recognized.

1.2. Performance-Related Reliability Measures

In reliability theory, several reliability measures have been proposed and used to evaluate a system (see Barlow and Proschan (1965, 1975)). In fault-tolerant computing, the following conventional reliability measures have been directly used:

  (i)   Reliability R(t).
  (ii)   Mean Time to First Failure (MTFF).
  (iii)   Mean Time Between Failures (MTBF).
  (iv)   Mean Down Time (MDT).
  (v)   Availabilities A(t) , A.

The above reliability measures are defined as follows: (i) The reliability R(t) is the probability of a system performing its functioning adequately for the intended period of time [0, t]. (ii) The MTFF is the mean time to first failure of a system, where failure means that the system cannot perform its functioning within the tolerances. (iii) The MTBF is the mean time between two successive failures of a system, where the system is repairable. Note that the MTFF can be applied to both an unrepairable system and a repairable system while the MTBF can be applied to only a repairable system. (iv) The MDT is the mean down time between two successive operations of a system, where, in general, the behavior of the repairable system repeats the MTBF and the MDT alternately. (v) The availability A(t) at time t is the probability that a system is active at time t within the tolerances. The availability A(t) is referred to as the 'pointwise availability' or the 'instantaneous availability.' The 'limiting availability' or the 'steady-state availability' (or just 'availability') is defined by $A \equiv \lim_{t \to \infty} A(t)$ when it exists.

If we consider the computer systems, we should consider the trade-off between the reliability and the performance. Under the same budget constraints of two different computer system configurations, the higher the reliability is, the lower the performance is. For instance, the performance of a dual system is less than that of a simplex system if we consider the simplex system and the corresponding dual system composed of the similar two units (processors). Therefore, we are very much interested in the gracefully degrading systems which balance the reliability with the performance. This chapter is mainly contributed to such the gracefully degrading systems from the viewpoint of the more generalized reliability measures. From these facts, the reliability measures defined above are not adequate for evaluating the computer systems since the performance is not taken into account in the reliability measures above.

Beaudry (1978) introduced the following performance-related reliability measures:

(vi)   The computation reliability $R^*(t, T)$.
(vii) The Mean Computation to First Failure (MCFF).
(viii) The computation thresholds t_T & T_t.
(ix)   The computation availabilities $A_c(t)$, A_c.
(x)   The capacity threshold t_c.

In particular, we cite the definitions of the above measures (vii), (ix), and (x) given by Beaudry (1978): (vii) The MCFF is the expected amount of computation available on a system before its first failure, given an initial system state. (ix) The computation availabilities $A_c(t)$ and A_c are the expected value of the computation capacity of a system at time t and in the steady-state (when it exists), respectively. (x) The capacity threshold t_c is the time at which the computation availability reaches a specific value.

Note that Beaudry (1978) called the Mean Computation Before Failure (MCBF) instead of the above measure (vii), the MCFF. However, we introduce a new measure:

(xi) The Mean Computation Between Failures (MCBF), which is defined as the expected amount of computation available on a system between two successive failures.

In this chapter, we use the MCBF as defined above in (xi) and use the MCFF as defined by the mean computation before failure given by Beaudry (1978).

In this chapter, we are mainly interested in the above measures (vii), (ix), (x), and (xi) and analyze the gracefully degrading systems by using both the probabilistic arguments (for unrepairable systems) and the Markov renewal processes (for repairable systems). Comparing the gracefully degrading systems with other systems such as a simplex system and a duplex system, we shall show the effectiveness balancing the performance with the reliability for the gracefully degrading systems.

1.3. Gracefully Degrading Systems (Unrepairable Systems)

Let us consider a gracefully degrading system composed of 2 units (processors), where the failed units are unrepairable. Each identical unit fails according to an arbitrary distribution $F(t)$ $(t \geq 0)$ with a finite mean $1/\lambda \equiv \int_0^\infty \bar{F}(t)dt$, where $\bar{F}(t) \equiv 1 - F(t)$. Once a faulty unit is detected, automatic reconfiguration is executed. We assume that the coverage α is the probability that the system reconfigures automatically given that the failed unit is detected, and the automatic switchover time is negligible. Then the system reliability can be obtained by the probabilistic arguments as follows: The probability that both units do not fail up to time t is $[\bar{F}(t)]^2$. The probability that one unit fails up to time t and the automatic recovery is suc-

cessful while another unit never fails up to time t is $2\alpha\bar{F}(t)F(t)$.
The above two events are mutually exclusive and exhaustive. Then

$$R(t) = \bar{F}(t)[\bar{F}(t) + 2\alpha F(t)] . \qquad (1.1)$$

Let us next consider the computation availability introduced by
Beaudry (1978). The computation capacity of a simplex system is assumed
to be unity, i.e., $c = 1$, when it is functioning. Then, the computation capacity of the gracefully degrading system is 2c when both units
are functioning correctly and c when only one unit is functioning
correctly. It is generally assumed that $c < 1$, i.e., that there is
some loss of performance due to parallel operation of both units. Then,
the computation availability of the gracefully degrading system is given
by

$$A_c(t) = 2c\bar{F}(t)[\bar{F}(t) + \alpha F(t)] . \qquad (1.2)$$

The MTFF is given by

$$MTFF = \int_0^\infty R(t)dt = \frac{2\alpha}{\lambda} + (1 - 2\alpha)\int_0^\infty [\bar{F}(t)]^2 dt . \qquad (1.3)$$

The Mean Computation to First Failure (MCFF) is given by integrating
the computation availability as follows:

$$MCFF = \int_0^\infty A_c(t)dt = 2c[\frac{\alpha}{\lambda} + (1 - \alpha)\int_0^\infty [\bar{F}(t)]^2 dt] . \qquad (1.4)$$

Note that Beaudry (1978) defined the above measure as the Mean Computation Before Failure (MCBF).   In this book, however, we should
define the Mean Computation Between Failures (MCBF) for repairable systems in the later section.
    If F(t) is assumed to be an exponential distribution (i.e.,
$\bar{F}(t) = e^{-\lambda t}$), then

$$MTFF = \frac{1 + 2\alpha}{2\lambda} , \qquad (1.5)$$

$$MCFF = \frac{1 + \alpha}{\lambda}c , \qquad (1.6)$$

which are coincident with those of Beaudry (1978).

If $F(t)$ is assumed to be a gamma distribution with shape parameter 2 (i.e., $\overline{F}(t) = (1 + 2\lambda t)e^{-2\lambda t}$), then

$$MTTF = \frac{5 + 6\alpha}{8\lambda} , \qquad (1.7)$$

$$MCFF = \frac{5 + 3\alpha}{4\lambda}c . \qquad (1.8)$$

We shall obtain the corresponding measures for a duplex system to compare with a gracefully degrading system considered above. The system reliability and the availability of the duplex system can be obtained as follows: The probability that the active unit does not fail up to time t is $\overline{F}(t)$. The probability that the active unit fails up to time t and, after that, the standby unit takes over its functioning at that time is $\alpha F(t)*\overline{F}(t)$, where, in general,

$$A(t)*B(t) \equiv \int_0^t A(t-x)dB(x) , \qquad (1.9)$$

is defined as the Stieltjes convolution of $A(t)$ and $B(t)$. The above two events are mutually exclusive and exhaustive. Then

$$R(t) = A(t) = \overline{F}(t) + \alpha F(t)*\overline{F}(t) , \qquad (1.10)$$

$$MTFF = MCFF = \frac{1 + \alpha}{\lambda} , \qquad (1.11)$$

where equation (1.11) depends on the mean $1/\lambda$, not on the distribution $F(t)$ itself.

Comparing (1.3) and (1.4) with (1.11), we see that the MTFF of the duplex system is greater than that of the gracefully degrading system. However, if

$$c > \frac{1 + \alpha}{2[\alpha + (1 - \alpha)\lambda\int_0^\infty [\overline{F}(t)]^2 dt]} \equiv D(\alpha) , \qquad (1.12)$$

then the MCFF of the gracefully degrading system is greater than that of the duplex system, and vice versa.

If we assume the exponential failure distribution, we have $D(\alpha) = 1$ which implies that the MCFF of the duplex system is greater than that of the gracefully degrading system. If we assume the gamma distribution with shape parameter 2 , we have

$$D(\alpha) = \frac{4(1 + \alpha)}{5 + 3\alpha} , \qquad (1.13)$$

which satisfies $4/5 < D(\alpha) < 1$. From (1.12), we see that there exists the possibility that the MCFF of the gracefully degrading system is greater than that of the duplex system. However, noting that

$$0 < \int_0^\infty [\overline{F}(t)]^2 dt < \int_0^\infty \overline{F}(t) dt \equiv 1/\lambda , \qquad (1.14)$$

and, even if (1.12) is held, the MCFF of the gracefully degrading system is not greater than $2/(1 + \alpha)$ times of that of the duplex system.

Let us consider the computation availability in (1.2) and (1.10). If $2c > 1$, then the computation availability of (1.2) is greater than that of (1.10) in the time $t < t_{MAX}$, where t_{MAX} satisfies

$$c = \frac{\overline{F}(t) + \alpha F(t)*\overline{F}(t)}{2\overline{F}(t)[\overline{F}(t) + \alpha F(t)]} \equiv H(\alpha, t) . \qquad (1.15)$$

Fig. 1.1 shows a graph of the computation availability versus the (dimensionless) time λt , where we assume the exponential distribution and the gamma distribution with shape parameter 2 for a simplex system, a duplex system, and a two-unit gracefully degrading system. Fig. 1.2 shows the dependence of the (dimensionless) time λt on the computation availability for a simplex system, a duplex system, and a two-unit gracefully degrading system, where $\alpha = 1$ and $\alpha = 0.8$. In general, we see from Fig. 1.2 that the improvement of the coverage is more effective when the duration of the system operation is longer.

Let us next consider an N-unit gracefully degrading system in general. Define that the state i $(i = 0, 1, 2, \ldots , N)$ represents the number of the failed units. The probability that the system is in state i at time t , given that the system was in state 0 at time 0, is given by

$$P_{0i}(t) = \binom{N}{i} [\alpha F(t)]^i [\overline{F}(t)]^{N-i} \qquad (i = 0, 1, 2, \ldots , N - 1).$$
$$\qquad (1.16)$$

Then the system reliability is given by

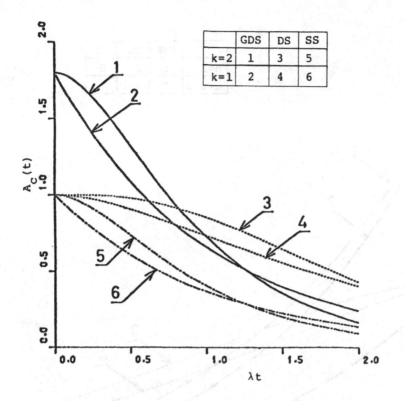

	GDS	DS	SS
k=2	1	3	5
k=1	2	4	6

GDS: Gracefully Degrading System
DS: Duplex System
SS: Simplex System

Fig. 1.1. The computation availability $A_c(t)$ versus (dimensionless) time λt for each system, where $\alpha = 0.99$, $c = 0.90$, and $k = 1$ (exponential distribution), 2 (gamma distribution).

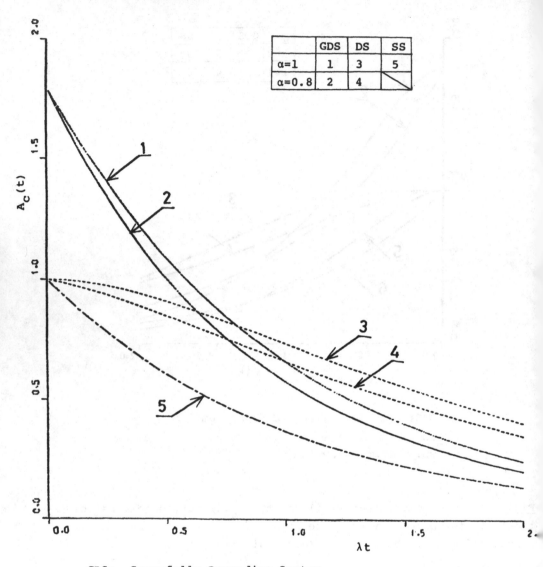

	GDS	DS	SS
α=1	1	3	5
α=0.8	2	4	

GDS: Gracefully Degrading System

DS: Duplex System

SS: Simplex System

<u>Fig. 1.2.</u>   The dependence of (dimensionless) time λt on the computation availability for each system, where $\alpha = 1$ and   0.8.

$$R(t) = \sum_{i=0}^{N-1} P_{0i}(t) = [\alpha F(t) + \overline{F}(t)]^N - [\alpha F(t)]^N . \tag{1.17}$$

Recall that state i represents the number of the failed units. We assume that the computation capacity in state i ($i = 0, 1, 2, \ldots$, $N - 1$) is $(N - i)c$ since the number of the remaining units in state i is $N - i$. Then the computation availability is given by

$$A_c(t) = \sum_{i=0}^{N-1} (N - i)c P_{0i}(t) . \tag{1.18}$$

The MTFF and the MCFF can be obtained from equations (1.17) and (1.18), respectively.

In particular, if we assume the exponential failure distribution (i.e., $\overline{F}(t) = e^{-\lambda t}$), then we have

$$MTFF = \frac{1}{\lambda} \sum_{i=1}^{N-1} \frac{\alpha^i}{N - i} , \tag{1.19}$$

$$MCFF = \frac{c}{\lambda} \cdot \frac{1 - \alpha^N}{1 - \alpha} , \tag{1.20}$$

which are coincident with the results by Beaudry (1978).

We shall obtain the corresponding measures for an N-unit standby redundant system. The probability that the system is in state i (i units have been failed) at time t , given that the system was in state 0 at time 0, is given by

$$P_{0i}(t) = \alpha^i [F(t)]^{i*} * \overline{F}(t) , \tag{1.21}$$

where $[F(t)]^{i*}$ is the i-fold Stieltjes convolution of F(t) with itself. Then the system reliability and the computation availability are given by

$$R(t) = A_c(t) = \sum_{i=0}^{N-1} \alpha^i [F(t)]^{i*} * \overline{F}(t) . \tag{1.22}$$

The MTFF and the MCFF of the N-unit standby redundant system are given by

$$MTFF = MCFF = \frac{1}{\lambda} \cdot \frac{1 - \alpha^N}{1 - \alpha} \ , \tag{1.23}$$

which depend only on the mean failure time $1/\lambda$, not on the distribution $F(t)$ itself.

Let us compare an N-unit gracefully degrading system with an N-unit standby redundant system, where the reliability measures are given in equations (1.17) - (1.23). We see that the MTFF of the standby redundant system is greater than that of the gracefully degrading system. We also see that the MTFF and the MCFF of the standby redundant system are greater than those of the simplex system. However, there exists the possibility that the MTFF and the MCFF of the gracefully degrading system are not greater than those of the simplex system if c and α are suitably chosen. We see that the computation availability of the gracefully degrading system is greater than that of the standby redundant system, if $N\alpha > 1$ and $t < t_{MAX}$, where t_{MAX} satisfies

$$c = \frac{\sum_{i=0}^{N-1} \alpha^i [F(t)]^{i*} * \bar{F}(t)}{N\bar{F}(t)[\alpha F(t) + \bar{F}(t)]^{N-1}} \equiv H(\alpha,t) \ . \tag{1.24}$$

Let t_0 be the duration of the system operation. If

$$c > H(\alpha, t_0) \ , \tag{1.25}$$

then we should apply the gracefully degrading system from the viewpoint of reliability.

In particular, if we assume the exponential distribution (i.e., $\bar{F}(t) = e^{-\lambda t}$), then we have

$$H(\alpha,t) = \frac{\sum_{i=0}^{N-1} (\alpha\lambda t)^i/i!}{N[\alpha + (1 - \alpha)e^{-\lambda t}]^{N-1}} \ . \tag{1.26}$$

It is difficult to solve the equation (1.24) analytically. However, it is fairly easy to solve it numerically. Fig. 1.3 shows a graph $H(\alpha,t)$ versus λt , where $\alpha = 0.7$ and $\alpha = 0.99$. From these curves in Fig. 1.3 , we see that $\lambda t_{MAX} < 1$ whenever $2c > 1$, which implies

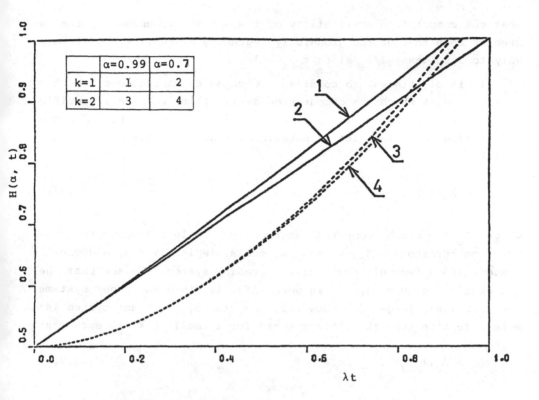

Fig. 1.3. A minimum capacity level c of the gracefully degrading system required to exceed the value of the computation availability of the standby redundant system as a function of time λt, where k = 1 (exponential distribution) and 2 (gamma distribution with shape parameter 2).

that the computation availability of the standby redundant system is greater than that of the gracefully degrading system, where t might vary to less than $1/\lambda$ since $t_{MAX} < 1/\lambda$.

It is of interest to consider the capacity threshold t_c which is the time at which the computation availability reaches a specific value since the computation availability is required to exceed a specific value ξ . Then the computation threshold is given by the solution to

$$\xi = A_c(t_c) , \qquad (1.27)$$

where $A_c(t)$ can be computed numerically. Table 1.1 shows the computation threshold λt_c versus ξ for a simplex system, a duplex system, and a two-unit gracefully degrading system. We see that the gracefully degrading system is more effective than the other systems for relatively large ξ . However, the standby redundant system is more effective than the other systems for a small $\xi < \xi_0$ such that

$$\xi_0 = A_c(t_{MAX}) . \qquad (1.28)$$

Fig. 1.4 shows a graph representing how to obtain the value ξ_0 from the computation capacity c , where we plot 2 curves $H(\alpha,t)$ and $A_c(t)$ versus λt simultaneously.

We have discussed a gracefully degrading system comparing with an unrepairable standby redundant system and an unrepairable simplex system. We conclude that the standby redundant system has the superior characteristics as far as the MTFF and the MCFF are concerned. However, if the duration of usage period is relatively short and the high computation capacity is required, the gracefully degrading system is considerably effective. We have discussed unrepairable systems throughout this section. If we specify t_0 as a usage period or a scheduled maintenance period, the results obtained in this section can be applied more extensively.

1.4. Gracefully Degrading Systems (Repairable Systems)

Consider a gracefully degrading system with repair facility. That is, a failed unit is repaired upon failure and recovers its func-

Table 1.1. The (dimensionless) capacity threshold $\lambda \cdot t_c$ versus ξ for the gracefully degrading system, the duplex system, and the simplex system, where $\overline{F}(t) = e^{-\lambda t}$, $c = 0.9$, and $\alpha = 0.99$.

ξ	$\lambda \cdot t_c$		
	GDS	DS	SS
0.999	0.5844	0.0365	0.0010
0.99	0.5934	0.1388	0.0101
0.9	0.6882	0.5219	0.1054
0.8	0.8054	0.8144	0.2231
0.7	0.9386	1.0873	0.3566

GDS: Gracefully Degrading System
DS: Duplex System
SS: Simplex System

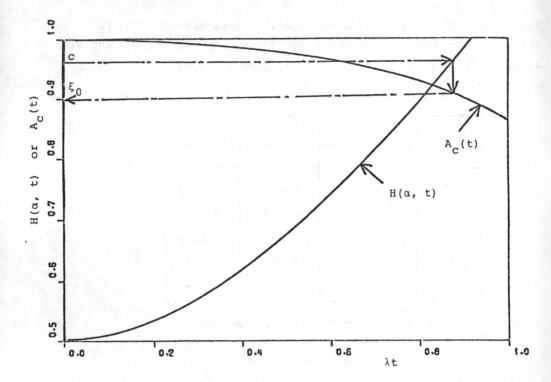

Fig. 1.4. The graph representing how to obtain the value of ξ_0 from the computation capacity c.

tioning after repair, where the repair includes fault-diagonosis, replacement and recovery. In this section we restricted ourselves to a two-unit gracefully degrading system because of its simplicity of analysis and of its wide application to real world.

Assume that the failure time of a single unit obeys an exponential distribution (i.e., $\bar{F}(t) = e^{-\lambda t}$). Assume also that the repair time of a failed unit obeys an arbitrary distribution $G(t)$ with mean $1/\mu \equiv \int_0^\infty \bar{G}(t)dt$. It is generally true that the probabilistic law of the repair time is not an exponential distribution but an arbitrary distribution such as a logarithmic normal distribution or a gamma distribution. We assume that the repair facility is a single and the repair discipline is 'first come, first served.'

To analyze a two-unit gracefully degrading system under the assumptions above, we introduce the following states (time instants) i $(i = 0, 1, 2, 3)$;

   state 0; both two units are operating,
   state 1; upon detection of a faulty unit, the repair of the faulty unit starts while the automatic switchover is successful,
   state 2; upon detection of a faulty unit, the repair of the faulty unit starts while the automatic switchover is failed (system break-down),
   state 3; an active unit fails while the faulty unit is under repair (system break-down),
where states 0, 1, and 2 are regeneration points while state 3 is a non-regeneration point.

Let us analyze the model above by using a Markov Renewal Process (MRP). If all the states defined above are regeneration points, it is quite easy to apply the conventional MRP's (see, e.g., Pyke (1961a, 1961b), Barlow and Proschan (1965)). However, we have to consider state 3 which is not a regeneration point in general (except the exponential repair time distribution, i.e., $\bar{G}(t) = e^{-\mu t}$). To overcome this difficulty, we can apply the unique modification of MRP's developed by Nakagawa and Osaki (1974). That is, we consider the one-step and two-step transition probabilities as follows:

$Q_{ij}(t)$ = Pr{after making a transition into state i, the process next makes a transition into state j, in an amount of time less than or equal to t },

$Q_{ij}^{(k)}(t) = \Pr\{$after making a transition into state i , the process next makes a transition into state j via state k , in an amount of time less than or equal to t $\}$,

where state i must be a regeneration point.

We have the following one-step and two-step transition probabilities:

$$Q_{01}(t) = \alpha \int_0^t (2\lambda) e^{-2\lambda t} dt \ , \tag{1.29}$$

$$Q_{02}(t) = (1 - \alpha) \int_0^t (2\lambda) e^{-2\lambda t} dt \ , \tag{1.30}$$

$$Q_{10}(t) = \int_0^t e^{-\lambda t} dG(t) \ , \tag{1.31}$$

$$Q_{13}(t) = \int_0^t \bar{G}(t) \lambda e^{-\lambda t} dt \ , \tag{1.32}$$

$$Q_{11}^{(3)}(t) = \int_0^t (1 - e^{-\lambda t}) dG(t) \ , \tag{1.33}$$

$$Q_{21}(t) = G(t) \ . \tag{1.34}$$

Let $q_{ij}(s)$ and $q_{ij}^{(k)}(s)$ denote the Laplace-Stieltjes (LS) transforms of $Q_{ij}(t)$ and $Q_{ij}^{(k)}(t)$, respectively. Then we have

$$q_{01}(s) = 2\lambda\alpha/(s + 2\lambda) \ , \tag{1.35}$$

$$q_{02}(s) = 2\lambda(1 - \alpha)/(s + 2\lambda) \ , \tag{1.36}$$

$$q_{10}(s) = g(s+\lambda) \ , \tag{1.37}$$

$$q_{13}(s) = \lambda[1 - g(s+\lambda)]/(s + \lambda), \tag{1.38}$$

$$q_{11}^{(3)}(s) = g(s) - g(s+\lambda) , \tag{1.39}$$

$$q_{21}(s) = g(s), \tag{1.40}$$

where $g(s)$ is the LS transform of $G(t)$.

Let $h_{OF}(s)$ denote the LS transform of the time distribution to first system break-down (i.e., state 2 or 3) starting from state 0. Then we have

$$h_{OF}(s) = \frac{q_{02}(s) + q_{01}(s)q_{13}(s)}{1 - q_{01}(s)q_{10}(s)} \; , \tag{1.41}$$

$$MTFF = \frac{1 + 2\alpha[1 - g(\lambda)]}{2\lambda[1 - \alpha g(\lambda)]} \; . \tag{1.42}$$

The MCFF is given by

$$MCFF = \frac{1 + \alpha[1 - g(\lambda)]}{\lambda[1 - \alpha g(\lambda)]}c \; . \tag{1.43}$$

Note that equations (1.42) and (1.43) are coincident with equations (1.5) and (1.6), respectively, as the mean repair time $1/\mu$ tends to zero.

The Mean Time Between Failures (MTBF) is one of the most important measures in reliability theory. The MTBF of the gracefully degrading system is given by

$$MTBF = \frac{2 - g(\lambda)}{2\lambda[1 - \alpha g(\lambda)]} \; . \tag{1.44}$$

We propose a new measure called the Mean Computation Between Failures (MCBF) which is the expected computation capacity between two successive failures. The MCBF of the gracefully degrading system is given by

$$MCBF = \frac{c}{\lambda[1 - \alpha g(\lambda)]} \; . \tag{1.45}$$

In particular, if we assume a gamma repair time distribution with shape parameter 2 (i.e., $\overline{G}(t) = (1 + 2\mu t)e^{-2\mu t}$), we have the improvement factor $\lambda \cdot MTFF$ of the MTFF for a two-unit gracefully degrading system to a simplex system as follows:

$$\lambda \cdot MTFF = \frac{4 + \rho(4 + \rho)(1 + 2\alpha)}{2[4(1 - \alpha) + \rho(4 + \rho)]} \; , \tag{1.46}$$

where $\rho \equiv \lambda/\mu$ is referred to as the <u>maintenance factor</u>. We have the similar improvement factors of the MCFF, MTBF, and MCBF for a gracefully degrading system to a simplex system as follows:

$$\lambda \cdot MCFF = \frac{4 + \rho(4 + \rho)(1 + \alpha)}{4(1 - \alpha) + \rho(4 + \rho)} c , \qquad (1.47)$$

$$\lambda \cdot MTBF = \frac{2 + \rho(4 + \rho)}{4(1 - \alpha) + \rho(4 + \rho)} , \qquad (1.48)$$

$$\lambda \cdot MCBF = \frac{(\rho + 2)^2}{4(1 - \alpha) + \rho(4 + \rho)} c . \qquad (1.49)$$

Figs. 1.5 - 1.8 show the graphs of the improvement factors $\lambda \cdot MTFF$, $\lambda \cdot MCFF$, $\lambda \cdot MTBF$, and $\lambda \cdot MCBF$ versus α when $\rho = 0.001$, 0.01 and 0.1 , respectively. From these figures, we see that the smaller the maintenance factor ρ is, the more effective each improvement factor is. However, we also see that the increase of the maintenance factor ρ from 0.01 to 0.001 is not essentially effective.

Consider the computation availability for the gracefully degrading system. Recall that the computation capacity is assumed to be 2c for sate 0 and c for state 1. We first derive the transition probability $P_{ij}(t)$ that the process is in state j at time t , given that it was in state i at time 0. Let $p_{ij}(s)$ denote the LS transform of $P_{ij}(t)$. Then we have

$$P_{00}(s) = [1 - q_{11}^{(3)}(s)][1 - q_{01}(s) - q_{02}(s)]/\Delta(s) , \qquad (1.50)$$

$$P_{01}(s) = [1 - q_{10}(s) - q_{13}(s)][q_{01}(s) + q_{02}(s)q_{21}(s)]/\Delta(s) , \qquad (1.51)$$

$$P_{02}(s) = q_{02}(s)[1 - q_{11}^{(3)}(s)][1 - q_{21}(s)]/\Delta(s) , \qquad (1.52)$$

$$P_{03}(s) = [q_{13}(s) - q_{11}^{(3)}(s)][q_{01}(s) + q_{02}(s)q_{21}(s)]/\Delta(s) , \qquad (1.53)$$

where

$$\Delta(s) \equiv 1 - q_{11}^{(3)}(s) - q_{10}(s)q_{01}(s) - q_{10}(s)q_{02}(s)q_{21}(s) . \qquad (1.54)$$

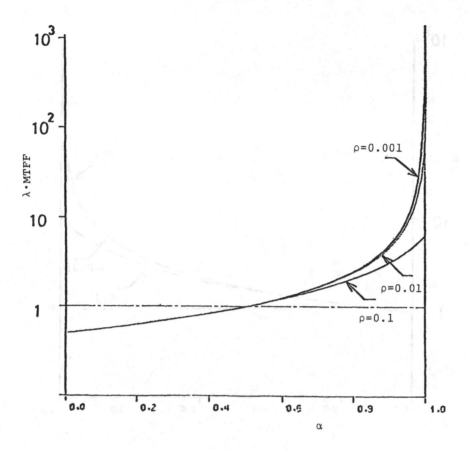

Fig. 1.5. The improvement factor $\lambda \cdot$MTFF for the two-unit gracefully degrading system to the simplex system.

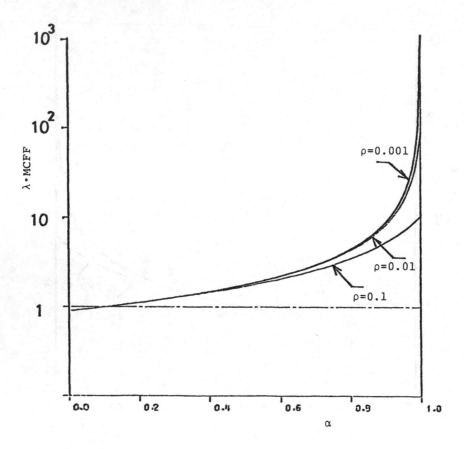

Fig. 1.6. The improvement factor $\lambda \cdot$MCFF for the two-unit gracefully degrading system to the simplex system.

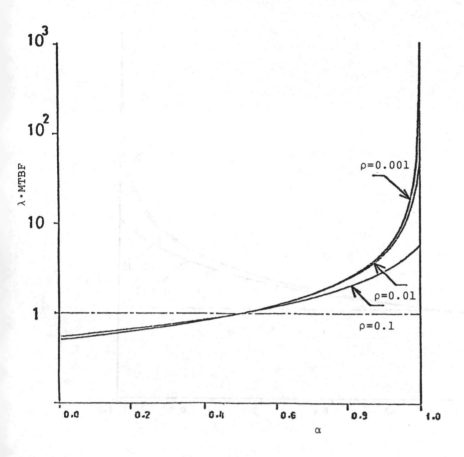

Fig. 1.7. The improvement factor λ·MTBF for the two-unit gracefully degrading system to the simplex system.

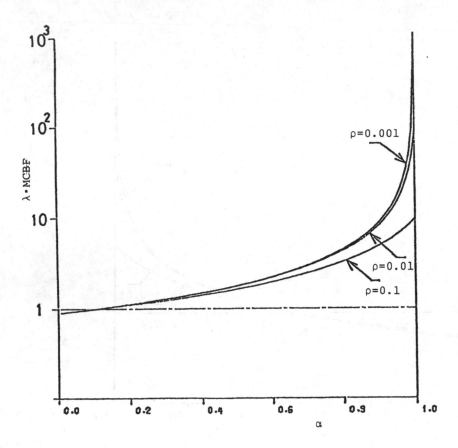

<u>Fig. 1.8.</u> The improvement factor $\lambda \cdot$ MCBF for the two-unit gracefully degrading system to the simplex system.

It is easy to verify that

$$\sum_{j=0}^{3} P_{0j}(s) = 1 . \tag{1.55}$$

It is very difficult to invert the LS transform $p_{ij}(s)$ except the simplest case of the exponential repair time distribution.

Let P_j denote the probability that the process is in state j in the steady-state, i.e.,

$$P_j = \lim_{t \to \infty} P_{0j}(t) = \lim_{s \to 0} p_{0j}(s) \qquad (j = 0, 1, 2, 3) , \tag{1.56}$$

which is independent of the initial state 0 under the suitable assumptions. Then we have

$$P_0 = \mu g(\lambda)/\Delta , \tag{1.57}$$

$$P_1 = 2\mu[1 - g(\lambda)]/\Delta , \tag{1.58}$$

$$P_2 = 2\lambda(1 - \alpha)g(\lambda)/\Delta , \tag{1.59}$$

$$P_3 = 2\{\lambda - \mu[1 - g(\lambda)]\}/\Delta , \tag{1.60}$$

where

$$\Delta \equiv 2\lambda + \{\mu + 2\lambda(1 - \alpha)\}g(\lambda) . \tag{1.61}$$

The availability and the computation availability are given by

$$A = P_0 + P_1 = \frac{[2 - g(\lambda)]\mu}{2\lambda + \{\mu + 2\lambda(1 - \alpha)\}g(\lambda)} , \tag{1.62}$$

$$A_c = 2cP_0 + cP_1 = \frac{2\mu c}{2\lambda + \{\mu + 2\lambda(1 - \alpha)\}g(\lambda)} . \tag{1.63}$$

In particular, if we assume the exponential repair time distribution (i.e., $\overline{G}(t) = e^{-\mu t}$), we have

$$A = \frac{(2\lambda + \mu)\mu}{2\lambda^2 + 2\lambda\mu(2 - \alpha) + \mu^2} , \tag{1.64}$$

$$A_c = \frac{2\mu(\lambda + \mu)}{2\lambda^2 + 2\lambda\mu(2 - \alpha) + \mu^2} c \; , \qquad (1.65)$$

which are coincident with those of Beaudry (1978).

If we assume the gamma distribution with shape parameter 2 (i.e., $\overline{G}(t) = (1 + 2\mu t)e^{-2\mu t}$), then we have

$$A = \frac{2 + \rho(4 + \rho)}{2 + 4\rho(1 - \alpha) + \rho(2 + \rho)^2} \; , \qquad (1.66)$$

$$A_c = \frac{(2 + \rho)^2 c}{2 + 4\rho(1 - \alpha) + \rho(2 + \rho)^2} \; , \qquad (1.67)$$

where $\rho \equiv \lambda/\mu$.

Fig. 1.9 shows the dependence of the coverage α to the computation availability when $\rho = 0.01$. The increase of the coverage from 70% to 99% implies that of the computation availability by about 0.56% in this example. Fig. 1.10 shows the dependence of the maintenance factor ρ to the computation availability when $\alpha = 0.7$ and 0.99 . We see from this figure that the greater the maintenance factor ρ is, the more effective the increase of the coverage α is. For instance, when $\rho = 0.1$, the increase of the coverage from 70% to 99% implies that of the computation availability by about 4.9% .

Let us derive the corresponding quantities above for a duplex system for comparison. We can easily obtain the MTFF, the MCFF, the MTBF, the MCBF, the availability, and the computation availability under the assumption that a standby unit never fails. We just give the following results:

$$\text{MTFF} = \text{MCFF} = \frac{1 + \alpha[1 - g(\lambda)]}{\lambda[1 - \alpha g(\lambda)]} \; , \qquad (1.68)$$

$$\text{MTBF} = \text{MCBF} = \frac{1}{\lambda[1 - \alpha g(\lambda)]} \; , \qquad (1.69)$$

$$A = A_c = \frac{\mu}{\lambda + \{\mu + \lambda(1 - \alpha)\}g(\lambda)} \; . \qquad (1.70)$$

Comparing equations (1.42) - (1.45) with equations (1.68) and (1.69), we see that the MTFF, the MCFF, the MTBF and the MCBF of the duplex system are greater than those of the gracefully degrading system. However, the computation availability of the gracefully degrading sys-

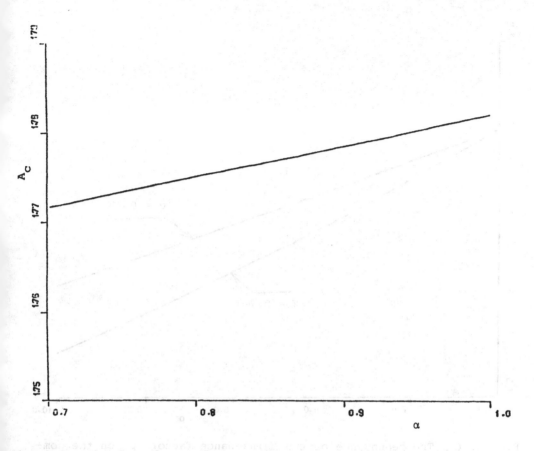

Fig. 1.9. The dependence of the coverage α on the computation availability for the two-unit gracefully degrading system, where ρ = 0.01.

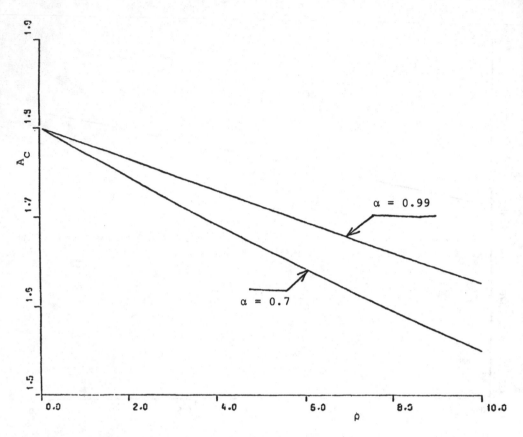

<u>Fig. 1.10.</u> The dependence of the maintenance factor ρ on the com-
putation availability for the two-unit gracefully degrading system,
where α =0.7 and 0.99.

tem is greater than that of the duplex system if

$$c > c_{MIN} \equiv \frac{2\lambda + \{\mu + 2\lambda(1 - \alpha)\}g(\lambda)}{2\lambda + 2\{\mu + \lambda(1 - \alpha)\}g(\lambda)} , \tag{1.71}$$

where c_{MIN} is a lower limit satisfying the above inequality. We define

$$\gamma \equiv c/c_{MIN} , \tag{1.72}$$

which denotes the improvement factor of the computation availability for a gracefully degrading system to a duplex system.

In particular, if we assume the gamma repair time distribution with shape parameter k (i.e., $\overline{G}(t) = \sum_{i=0}^{k} (k\mu t)^i e^{-k\mu t}/i!$), then we have

$$c_{MIN} = \frac{2\rho + [1 + 2\rho(1 - \alpha)][k/(\rho + k)]^k}{2\rho + 2[1 + \rho(1 - \alpha)][k/(\rho + k)]^k} . \tag{1.73}$$

It is noted that $k = 1$ implies the exponential distribution and $k \to \infty$ implies the unit step function at $t = 1/\mu$.

Fig. 1.11 shows the dependence of the coverage α to the minimum level c_{MIN} in the gracefully degrading system required to exceed the computation availability of the duplex system when ρ varies. We see that the dependence of the coverage α is a little when ρ is relatively small.

Fig. 1.12 shows the dependence of the maintenance factor ρ on the minimum level c_{MIN} for the gracefully degrading system required to exceed the computation availability of the duplex system when $k = 1, 2,$ and $\alpha = 0.70, 0.99$. We see from this figure that the dependence of ρ is relatively large. However, the dependence of $k = 1$ or 2 is gradually larger when ρ is greater. In computer systems, we may assume $\rho \ll 1$, in general, which implies no dependence of the repair time distribution. Thus, we have the following approximation formula:

$$c_{MIN} \approx \frac{1 - (3 - 2\rho)\rho}{2[1 + \rho(1 - \alpha)]} . \tag{1.74}$$

Fig. 1.13 shows the true value c_{MIN} and the approximation formula in (1.74). We see that the approximation formula in (1.74) is quite good when $\rho \ll 1$.

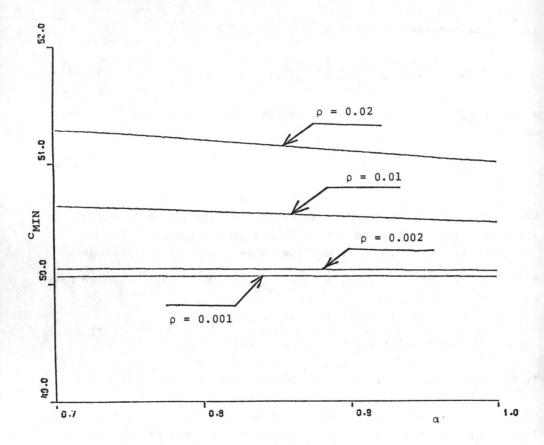

Fig. 1.11. The dependence of the coverage α on the minimum level c_{MIN} for the two-unit gracefully degrading system required to exceed the value of the computation availability of the duplex system, where ρ = 0.001, 0.002, 0.01, and 0.02.

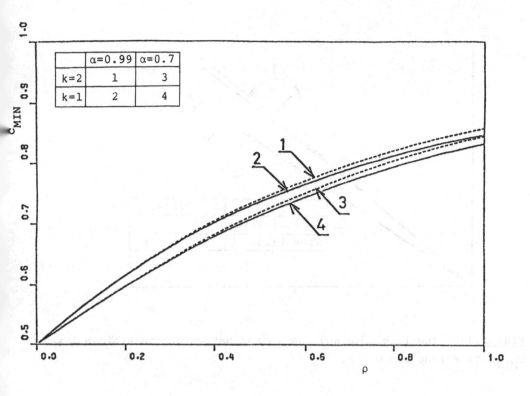

Fig. 1.12. The dependence of the maintenance factor ρ on the minimum
level c_{MIN} for the two-unit gracefully degrading system required to
exceed the value of the computation availability of the duplex system,
where $\alpha = 0.7$, 0.99, and $k = 1, 2$.

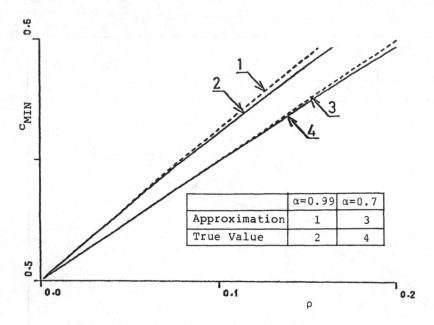

Fig. 1.13. The true value and the approximation of the minimum level c_{MIN} as a function of ρ.

Fig. 1.14 shows the improvement factor γ of the gracefully degrading system to the duplex system as a function of ρ when $k = 2$.
We see that the gracefully degrading system is very effective when
ρ is small.

We conclude that the MTFF, the MCFF, the MTBF, the MCBF and the
availability of the duplex system are greater than those of the gracefully degrading system. However, the computation availability of the
gracefully degrading system is greater than that of the duplex system
if equation (1.71) is satisfied. The computation availability is one
of the most important measures which balances the reliability with the
performance in computer systems. We have applied the computation availability as a criterion of the performance-related reliability measures
in this chapter.

In this section we have discussed a two-unit gracefully degrading
system and compared with a duplex system. It is of great interest
that the comparisons between two systems depend on the reliability and
the performance-related reliability measures we apply. In particular,
it is of great importance to apply the performance-related reliability
measures for computer systems.

We have restricted a two-unit gracefully degrading system. In
the later chapter we shall discuss a three-unit hybrid redundant system
which is composed of a two-unit gracefully degrading system and a
standby redundant unit.

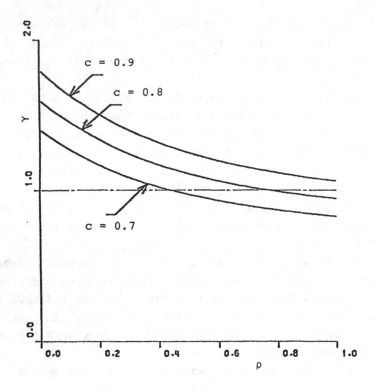

Fig. 1.14. The dependence of the maintenance factor ρ on the improvement factor γ for the two-unit gracefully degrading system to the duplex system.

CHAPTER 2

RELIABILITY ANALYSIS OF SOME COMPUTER ARCHITECTURES

2.1. Introduction

A fault-tolerant computer system with high reliability can be
achieved both by hardware and software which employ some kinds of
redundancy such as static redundancy (masking redundancy), dynamic
redundancy (see Short (1968)), software redundancy (see Randell (1975)),
and time (execution)redundancy (see Avizienis (1976)). In this chapter,
we are interested in the ultra-reliable computer systems from the viewpoint of hardware, i.e., system configuration by hardware dynamic
redundancy (usually supported by software and time redundancy techniques).

There are three typical system configurations to achieve high reliability, which can be applied to a vehicle traffic control system,
a seat reservation system, an on-line real time banking system, a
communication system and so on. That is, (1) a duplex system; a two-unit
standby redundant system, which employs two functionally identical
sub-systems where one is used to perform the functioning, the other is
waiting to be switched in against the active sub-system failure, (2)
a dual system; a two-unit parallel redundant system, which employs
two functionally identical sub-systems which execute identical tasks
for the purpose of comparing the outputs, and (3) a multi system (a
gracefully degrading system), which employs some functional processors
using common resources, attempts to reconfigure to a system without the
failure module in against the active module failure.

The purpose of this chapter is to investigate the availability and
the Mean Time Between Failures (MTBF) for each model. We introduce
three models composed of 4 units for each system, and introduce further
a model which represents a non-redundant system composed of 2 units,
to compare the above ultra-reliable systems. We obtain the availability
and the MTBF for each model by applying the unique modification of
Markov Renewal Processes (MRP's). It is commonly true to consider both
the availability and the MTBF in the commercial computer systems since

the system break-down for a short time can be allowed in general.

2.2. Models

Assumptions

Introduce the following assumptions common to the models below unless otherwise specified:

(i)   Each system is composed of 4 units, i.e., units A_i ($i = 1,2$) and units B_i ($i = 1,2$). Units A_1 and A_2 are identical processing units. Units B_1 and B_2 are identical storage units.

(ii)   Units A_i ($i = 1,2$) and B_i ($i = 1,2$) obey the exponential failure time distributions with rates λ_1 and λ_2, respectively, except the duplex system. For the duplex system, units A_1 and B_1 obey the exponential failure time distributions with rates λ_1 and λ_2, respectively, if a pair of units A_1 and B_1 forms on-line sub-system, and units A_2 and B_2 obey the exponential failure time distributions with rates $a\lambda_1$ and $a\lambda_2$ ($0 \leq a \leq 1$), respectively, if a pair of units A_2 and B_2 forms off-line sub-system, and vice versa.

(iii)   Units A_i ($i = 1, 2$) and B_i ($i = 1, 2$) obey the arbitray repair time distributions $G_1(t)$ and $G_2(t)$ with means $1/\gamma_1$ and $1/\gamma_2$, respectively.

(iv)   The repair facility is a single and the repair discipline is 'first come, first served.'

(v)   Each switchover is perfect and instantaneous.

Notation

Introduce the following notations for analysis of each model:

$\underline{U}_i$	; a set of all states for model i,
$\underline{R}_i$	; a set of regeneration points for model i,
$g_i(s)$	; Laplace-Stieltjes (LS) transform of $G_i(t)$,
NR_i	; a set of non-regeneration points for model i,
$\underline{A}_i$	; a set of operating states for model i,
$\underline{Q}_i$	; limiting transition probability matrix composed of the

possible regeneration points for model i,

A_i ; limiting availability for model i,

B_i ; MTBF for model i,

F_i ; the expected number of occurring the system break-down per unit of time in the steady-state,

$\theta_a \equiv \lambda_1 + \lambda_2 + a(\lambda_1 + \lambda_2)$,

$\theta_1 \equiv \lambda_1 + 2\lambda_2$,

$\theta_2 \equiv 2\lambda_1 + \lambda_2$,

$[\cdot]'|_{s=0} \equiv \lim_{s \to 0} d[\cdot]/ds$.

Model 1 (Simplex System)

Consider a model of the simplex system in Fig. 2.1. The simplex system is introduced to compare with ultra-reliable computer systems. Units A_1 and B_1 form the system, and the system cannot perform its functioning whenever one of two units fails, i.e., only unit A_1 or B_1 cannot execute tasks. This system is a fundamental fault-intolerant computer system, which is generally used as a batch system.

Introduce the following states (time instants) i (i ϵ $\underline{U}_1$ = { 0, 1, 2}) for this model;

state 0; system is operating,
state 1; unit A_1 fails (system break-down),
state 2; unit B_1 fails (system break-down),

where state means the status of the system and time instant means the time instant at which the process just enters the state. Then we can show the state transition diagram among the states above in Fig. 2.2.

Model 2 (Duplex System and Dual System)

Consider two models of redundant systems which employ two identical-ly functional sub-systems, where one is used actively to perform the functioning and another waiting to be switched in (or actively to perform the identical functioning) against the active sub-system failure. That is, we can consider the following two cases of standby (or parallel) redundancy.

Model 2-a (Duplex System): One sub-system functions as on-line sub-system and another as off-line sub-system which is in standby for on

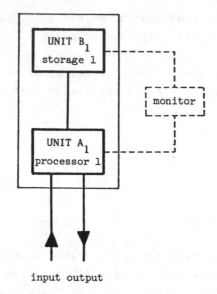

input output

Fig. 2.1. A basic configuration of a simplex system.

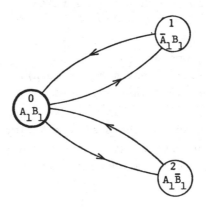

Fig. 2.2. State transition diagram among the states of the simplex system (model 1), where ' ◯ ' represents a state with regeneration point, ' ⬤ ' represents an operating state, '‾' represents that the unit is under repair.

-line. This system is capable of attaining ultra-reliability as using
high reliable units having static redundancy (masking redundancy), e.g.,
triple-modular redundancy (see Avizienis (1976)) and N-modular redundancy (see Mathur and Avizienis (1970)). We assume that each pair of
units A_i and B_i (i = 1 or 2) forms on-line sub-system and another pair
of units A_j and B_j (j = 1 or 2) forms off-line sub-system, and the
system can perform its functioning when either sub-system functions
(see Fig. 2.3).

Model 2-b (Dual System): Both sub-systems function as on-line sub
-systems and execute identical tasks for the purpose of comparing the
outputs, i.e., this system can avoid to occur the wrong outputs, and
still can continue to function even if one sub-system should fail without only a little interrupted time (in the duplex system, if the on
-line sub-system fails, the system needs error correction which can be
attained by recomputation retracing to a 'rollback' point of program
segments of entire programs). We assume that two pairs of units A_i and
B_i (i = 1, 2) form two sub-systems, respectively, and the system can
perform its functioning when either sub-system functions (see Fig. 2.4).
    The models above have different functions, however, the behaviors
for failure and repair under the assumptions (i) - (v) are the same.
Hence, we introduce the following states (time instants) i (i ε $\underline{U}_2$ =
{ 0, 1, ..,, 6});

    state 0; both sub-systems are operating,
    state 1; unit A_i (i = 1 or 2) fails, i.e., one sub-system fails,
             the failed unit is repaired immediately and the system
             is functioning only with one sub-system,
    state 2; unit B_i (i = 1 or 2) fails, then the behavior of the
             system is the same as state 1,
    state 3; unit A_i (i = 1 or 2) fails through state 1 (system break
             -down),
    state 4; unit B_i (i = 1 or 2) fails through state 1 (system break
             -down),
    state 5; unit A_i (i = 1 or 2) fails through state 2 (system break
             -down),
    state 6; unit B_i (i = 1 or 2) fails through state 2 (system break
             -down),

where states i (i ε $\underline{R}_2$ = {0, 1, 2}) are regeneration points and states
i (i ε $\underline{NR}_2$ = {3, 4, 5, 6}) are non-regeneration points. Then we can
show the state transition diagram among the states above in Fig. 2.5.

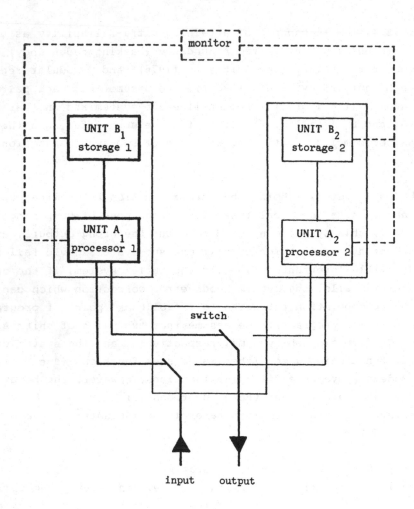

Fig. 2.3.   A basic configuration of a duplex system.

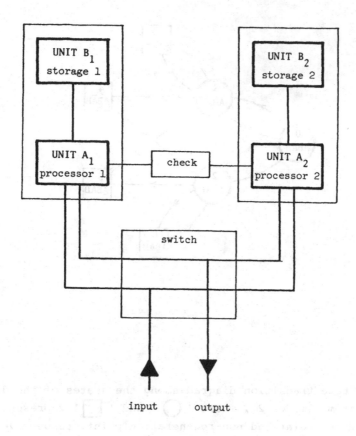

Fig. 2.4. A basic configuration of a dual system.

42

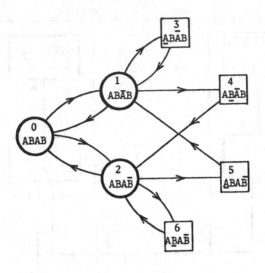

<u>Fig. 2.5.</u> State transition diagram among the states of the duplex and
the dual systems (model 2), where ' ◯ ' and ' ▢ ' represent states
with regeneration point and non-regeneration point, respectively,
' ⬤ ' represents an operating state, '‾' and '_' represent that the
unit is under repair and that the unit is waiting for repair, respectively, and 'A' and 'B' represent unit A_i (i = 1 or 2) and unit B_i
(i = 1 or 2), respectively.

Model 3 (Multi System)

Consider a model of the multi system shown in Fig. 2.6. The system is composed of 4 units, A_i (i = 1, 2) and B_i (i = 1, 2), and usually requires all the units for executing on-line tasks. However, when a unit failure is detected, the system may continue to operate without the failed unit, i.e., the remaining units attempt to reconfigure to a system reducing to the system performance and reliability. Hence, the system can perform its functioning if any combination of units A_i (i = 1, 2) and B_i (i = 1, 2) may do. If two units A_i (i = 1 and 2) or B_i (i = 1 and 2) are under failure simultaneously, the system break-down takes place.

This system requires very complex software and hardware, but may have the high performance for computation and ultra-reliability with the assistance of the hardware techniques, i.e., static redundancy (see, e.g.,Short (1968)) and self-repair (see Avizienis et al. (1971)), and so on, and of the software technique, i.e., software redundancy (see Randell (1975)) and so on. A typical system is the multi processor system (see, e.g., Hopkins and Smith (1975)), which is used for an on-line real time system.

Considering the above model, we introduce the following states (time instants) i (i $\in$ $\underline{U}_3$ = {0, 1, ..., 14}) on the basis of the assumptions defined above;

state 0; all units are operating,
state 1; unit A_i (i = 1 or 2) fails,
state 2; unit B_i (i = 1 or 2) fails,
state 3; unit B_i (i = 1 or 2) fails through state 1,
state 4; unit A_i (i = 1 or 2) fails through state 2,
state 5; unit A_i (i = 1 or 2) fails through state 1 (system break
          -down),
state 6; unit B_i (i = 1 or 2) fails through state 2 (system break
          -down),
state 7; unit A_i (i = 1 or 2) fails through state 3 or state 12
          (system break-down),
state 8; unit B_i (i = 1 or 2) fails through state 4 or state 11
          (system break-down),
state 9; unit B_i (i = 1 or 2) fails through state 3 or state 12
          (system break-down),
state 10; unit A_i (i = 1 or 2) fails through state 4 or state 11
          (system break-down),

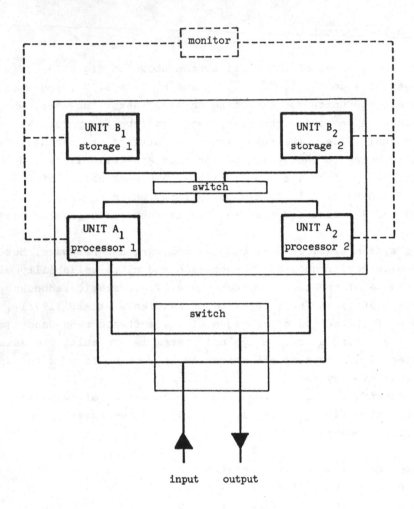

Fig. 2.6. A basic configuration of a multi system.

state 11; the repair of unit A_i (i = 1 or 2) is completed through
state 7,

state 12; the repair of unit B_i (i = 1 or 2) is completed through
state 8,

state 13; the repair of unit A_i (i = 1 or 2) is completed through
state 9,

state 14; the repair of unit B_i (i = 1 or 2) is completed through
state 10,

where states i ($i \in \underline{R}_3 = \{0, 1, 2, 11, 12, 13, 14\}$) are regeneration
points and states i ($i \in \underline{NR}_3 = \{3, 4, 5, 6, 7, 8, 9, 10\}$) are non-regeneration points. Then we can show the state transition diagram among the
states above in Fig. 2.7.

2.3. Availability and MTBF

Let us describe the procedure of analysis by using MRP's for each
model mentioned above. If all the states defined above are regeneration
points, it is quite easy to apply the conventional MRP's (see, e.g.,
Pyke (1961a), (1961b), and Barlow and Proschan (1965).). However, we
have to consider some states which are not regeneration points since
we assume the arbitrary repair time distributions for each model. To
overcome this difficulty, we can apply the unique modification of MRP's
developed by Nakagawa and Osaki (1974). That is, if we consider the
transition from state i to state j, where the starting state i is a
regeneration point, we can obtain the one-step transition probability
$Q_{ij}(t)$ (see Pyke (1961a)). However, since the starting states k and ℓ are
not regeneration points, we introduce the two-step transition probability $Q_{ij}^{(k)}(t)$ or the three-step transition probability $Q_{ij}^{(k,\ell)}(t)$, where
state i must be a regeneration point. That is, we can summarize the
definitions of the transition probabilities as follows:

$Q_{ij}(t)$　　　　= Pr{after making a transition into state i, the process
　　　　　　　　next makes a transition into state j, in an amount
　　　　　　　　of time less than or equal to t}.

$Q_{ij}^{(k)}(t)$　　　= Pr{after making a transition into state i, the process
　　　　　　　　next makes a transition into state j via state k,
　　　　　　　　in an amount of time less than or equal to t}.

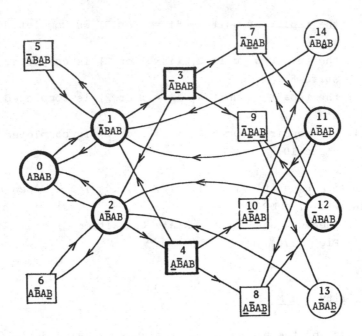

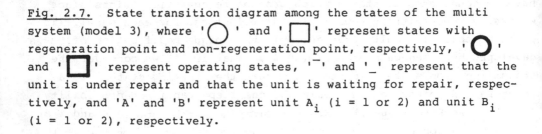

Fig. 2.7. State transition diagram among the states of the multi system (model 3), where '◯' and '☐' represent states with regeneration point and non-regeneration point, respectively, '⬤' and '◼' represent operating states, '⁻' and '_' represent that the unit is under repair and that the unit is waiting for repair, respectively, and 'A' and 'B' represent unit A_i (i = 1 or 2) and unit B_i (i = 1 or 2), respectively.

$Q_{ij}^{(k,\ell)}(t)$ = Pr{after making a transition into state i, the process next makes a transition into state j via states k and ℓ, in an amount of time less than or equal to t}.

We can apply the unique modification of MRP's using the transition probabilities $Q_{ij}(t)$, $Q_{ij}^{(k)}(t)$, and $Q_{ij}^{(k,\ell)}(t)$ based on the regeneration point techniques. A detailed discussion of this technique will be founded in a paper by Nakagawa and Osaki (1974).

We review the procedure of analysis, where we assume that the number of all states is n:

(i) Derive the transition probabilities $Q_{ij}(t)$, $Q_{ij}^{(k)}(t)$, and $Q_{ij}^{(k,\ell)}(t)$ for all states considered using the states defined above.

(ii) Taking the LS transforms for $Q_{ij}(t)$, $Q_{ij}^{(k)}(t)$, and $Q_{ij}^{(k,\ell)}(t)$ yields the LS transforms $q_{ij}(s)$, $q_{ij}^{(k)}(s)$, and $q_{ij}^{(k,\ell)}(s)$, respectively.

(iii) Assume the limiting transition probabilities as follows:

$$q_{ij} \equiv \lim_{s \to 0} q_{ij}(s), \tag{2.1}$$

$$q_{ij}^{(k)} \equiv \lim_{s \to 0} q_{ij}^{(k)}(s), \tag{2.2}$$

$$q_{ij}^{(k,\ell)} \equiv \lim_{s \to 0} q_{ij}^{(k,\ell)}(s), \tag{2.3}$$

and solve for the limiting probabilities π_i (i = 0, ..., m), which denote the probability of being in state i after an infinite number of transitions have occurred (see, e.g., Barlow and Proschan (1965)) for the embedded <u>Markov Chain</u> (MC):

$$\underline{\pi} = \underline{\pi} \cdot \underline{Q} \text{ and } \sum_{k=0}^{m} \pi_k = 1, \tag{2.4}$$

where $\underline{\pi} = [\pi_0, \pi_1, ..., \pi_m]$ is a row vector and $\underline{Q}$ is a transition probability matrix composed of the possible regeneration points i = 0, 1, ..., m, i.e., neglecting the non-regeneration points and relabeling i = 0, 1, ..., m only for the possible regeneration points:

$$
\underline{Q} = \begin{pmatrix} \tilde{q}_{00} & \tilde{q}_{01} & \cdots & \tilde{q}_{0m} \\ \tilde{q}_{10} & \tilde{q}_{11} & \cdots & \tilde{q}_{1m} \\ \vdots & & \ddots & \vdots \\ \tilde{q}_{m0} & \tilde{q}_{m1} & \cdots & \tilde{q}_{mm} \end{pmatrix} , \tag{2.5}
$$

where $\tilde{q}_{ij}$ can be obtained by neglecting the non-regeneration points.

(iv)   Derive the unconditional means μ_i ($i = 0, 1, \ldots, m$), which denote the mean sojourn time of the process in state i (see, e.g., Barlow and Proschan (1965)), neglecting the non-regeneration points.

(v)   Calculate the mean recurrence times from state i to state i (see Barlow and Proschan (1965)) as follows:

$$
\ell_{ii} = \sum_{k=0}^{m} \pi_k \mu_k / \pi_i \qquad (i = 0, 1, \ldots, m). \tag{2.6}
$$

(vi)   Derive the unconditional means ξ_i ($i = 0, 1, \ldots, n$) not neglecting the non-regeneration points.

(vii)   Calculate the limiting probabilities p_i ($i = 0, 1, \ldots, n$) using the mean recurrence times and the unconditional means.

(viii)   The limiting availability A_i (for model i) can be obtained by summing up the limiting probabilities for the operating states.

(ix)   Obtain F_i (for model i) which is the expected numbers of occurring the system break-down per unit of time in the steady-state, using the mean recurrence times and the limiting probabilities.

(x)   The MTBF B_i (for model i) can be obtained as follows:

$$
B_i = A_i / F_i . \tag{2.7}
$$

Model 1 (Simplex System)

Consider a model of the simplex system. We can easily obtain the limiting availability and the MTBF by applying the conventional MRP's since the states defined in Section 2.2 are all the regeneration points

We derive the transition probabilities $Q_{ij}(t)$ ($i, j \in \underline{U}_1$) and take the LS transforms for those, respectively.   Then

$$q_{0i}(s) = \lambda_i/(s + \theta_0) \qquad (i = 1, 2) , \qquad (2.8)$$

$$q_{i0}(s) = g_i(s) \qquad (i = 1, 2) . \qquad (2.9)$$

Using the results, we can obtain the following limiting availability for the simplex system:

$$A_1 = \mu_0/\ell_{00} = (\lambda_1/\gamma_1 + \lambda_2/\gamma_2 + 1)^{-1}, \qquad (2.10)$$

where μ_0 is the unconditional mean for state 0 given by

$$\mu_0 = [1 - q_{01}(s) - q_{02}(s)]^{\prime}|_{s=0} = 1/\theta_0 \equiv 1/(\lambda_1 + \lambda_2), \qquad (2.11)$$

and ℓ_{00} is the mean recurrence time for state 0 given by

$$\ell_{00} = [1 - q_{01}(s)q_{10}(s) - q_{02}(s)q_{20}(s)]^{\prime}|_{s=0}$$

$$= (1/\theta_0)(\lambda_1/\gamma_1 + \lambda_2/\gamma_2 + 1). \qquad (2.12)$$

We further obtain the MTBF:

$$B_1 = 1/\theta_0. \qquad (2.13)$$

Model 2 (Duplex System and Dual System)

Consider the model 2-a and the model 2-b for the duplex system and the dual system, respectively. The difference of analysis between the model 2-a (duplex system) and the model 2-b (dual system) is only the failure rates. In the model 2-a, the failure rates for standby units A_i and B_i ($i = 1$ or 2) are $a\lambda_1$ and $a\lambda_2$, respectively. However, in the model 2-b, the failure rates for units A_i and B_i ($i = 1$ and 2) are always λ_1 and λ_2, respectively, i.e., $a = 1$, since they are in parallel. Hence, we can similarly analyze both the models 2-a and 2-b, where, in general, the failure rates are $a\lambda_1$ and $a\lambda_2$ for standby units A_i and B_i ($i = 1$ or 2), respectively.

We first derive the transition probabilities $Q_{ij}(t)$ ($i \in \underline{R}_2$, $j \in \underline{U}_2$) and $Q_{ij}^{(k)}(t)$ ($i \in \underline{R}_2$, $k \in \underline{NR}_2$, $j \in \underline{U}_2$), and take the LS transforms for those, respectively. Then

$$q_{0i}(s) = (1 + a)\lambda_i/(s + \theta_a) \qquad (i = 1, 2), \qquad (2.14)$$

$$q_{i0}(s) = g_i(s + \theta_0) \qquad (i = 1, 2), \qquad (2.15)$$

$$q_{i,j+2\times i}(s) = [\lambda_j/(s + \theta_0)][1 - g_i(s + \theta_0)] \qquad (i, j = 1, 2), \qquad (2.16)$$

$$q_{i,j}^{(j+2\times i)}(s) = [\lambda_j/(s + \theta_0)][g_i(s) - g_i(s + \theta_0)] \qquad (i, j = 1, 2). \qquad (2.17)$$

Using the above results and noting that states 0, 1, and 2 are the regeneration points, we have the following transition probability matrix $\underline{Q}_2$ for the embedded MC:

$$\underline{Q}_2 = \begin{pmatrix} 0 & q_{01} & q_{02} \\ q_{10} & q_{11}^{(3)} & q_{12}^{(4)} \\ q_{20} & q_{22}^{(6)} & q_{21}^{(5)} \end{pmatrix}, \qquad (2.18)$$

where

$$q_{0i} = (1 + a)\lambda_i/\theta_a \qquad (i = 1, 2), \qquad (2.19)$$

$$q_{i0} = g_i(\theta_0) \qquad (i = 1, 2), \qquad (2.20)$$

$$q_{i,j}^{(j+2\times i)} = (\lambda_j/\theta_0)[1 - g_i(\theta_0)] \qquad (i, j = 1, 2). \qquad (2.21)$$

Solving the following equations, we can obtain the limiting probabilities π_i ($i \in \underline{R}_2$) for the embedded MC:

$$[\pi_0, \pi_1, \pi_2] = [\pi_0, \pi_1, \pi_2]\underline{Q}_2 \qquad \text{and} \qquad \sum_{k \in \underline{R}_2} \pi_k = 1. \qquad (2.22)$$

The unconditional means μ_i ($i \in \underline{R}_2$) neglecting the non-regeneration points are given by

$$\mu_0 = [1 - q_{01}(s) - q_{02}(s)]'|_{s=0} = 1/\theta_a, \qquad (2.23)$$

$$\mu_i = [1 - q_{i0}(s) - q_{i,1}^{(1+2\times i)}(s) - q_{i,2}^{(2+2\times i)}(s)]'|_{s=0}$$

$$= 1/\gamma_i \qquad\qquad (i = 1, 2). \qquad\qquad (2.24)$$

Then we calculate the mean recurrence times:

$$\ell_{ii} = \sum_{k\epsilon \underline{R}_2} \pi_k \mu_k / \pi_i \qquad\qquad (i \epsilon \underline{R}_2). \qquad\qquad (2.25)$$

The unconditional means ξ_i ($i \epsilon \underline{A}_2$) not neglecting the non-regeneration points are given by

$$\xi_0 = \mu_0 = 1/\theta_a , \qquad\qquad (2.26)$$

$$\xi_i = [1 - q_{i0}(s) - q_{i,1+2\times i}(s) - q_{i,2+2\times i}(s)]'|_{s=0}$$

$$= (1/\theta_0)[1 - g_i(\theta_0)] \qquad\qquad (i = 1, 2). \qquad\qquad (2.27)$$

From the above results we calculate the limiting probabilities for operating states:

$$P_i = \xi_i / \ell_{ii} \qquad\qquad (i \epsilon \underline{A}_2). \qquad\qquad (2.28)$$

Thus, we obtain the limiting availability:

$$A_2 = \sum_{k\epsilon\underline{A}_2} P_k . \qquad\qquad (2.29)$$

We further obtain the expected number of occurring the system break -down per unit of time in the steady-state:

$$F_2 = \sum_{k=1}^{2} (q_{k,1+2\times k} + q_{k,2+2\times k})/\ell_{kk} . \qquad\qquad (2.30)$$

From the results above we obtain the MTBF:

$$B_2 = A_2/F_2 . \qquad\qquad (2.31)$$

Model 3 (Multi System)

Consider a model of the multi system. We first derive the transition probabilities $Q_{ij}(t)$ ($i \epsilon \underline{R}_3$, $j \epsilon \underline{U}_3$), $Q_{ij}^{(k)}(t)$ ($i \epsilon \underline{R}_3$, $k \epsilon \underline{NR}_3$,

$j \in \underline{U}_3$), and $Q_{ij}^{(k,\ell)}(t)$ ($i \in \underline{R}_3$, k and $\ell \in \underline{NR}_3$, $j \in \underline{U}_3$), respectively, and take the LS transforms for those. However, we omit the results here. From the results we obtain the following limiting transition probability matrix $\underline{Q}_3$ for the embedded MC:

$$
\underline{Q}_3 = \begin{pmatrix}
0 & q_{01} & q_{02} & 0 & 0 & 0 & 0 \\
q_{10} & q_{11}^{(5)} & q_{12}^{(3)} & q_{1,11}^{(3,7)} & 0 & q_{1,13}^{(3,9)} & 0 \\
q_{20} & q_{21}^{(4)} & q_{22}^{(6)} & 0 & q_{2,12}^{(4,8)} & 0 & q_{2,14}^{(4,10)} \\
0 & q_{11,1} & 0 & 0 & q_{11,12}^{(8)} & 0 & q_{11,14}^{(10)} \\
0 & 0 & q_{12,2} & q_{12,11}^{(7)} & 0 & q_{12,13}^{(9)} & 0 \\
0 & 0 & q_{13,2} & 0 & 0 & 0 & 0 \\
0 & q_{14,1} & 0 & 0 & 0 & 0 & 0
\end{pmatrix} ,
$$

$$(2.32)$$

where

$$q_{0i} = \lambda_i/\theta_0 \qquad (i = 1, 2), \qquad (2.33)$$

$$q_{i0} = g_i(\theta_i) \qquad (i = 1, 2), \qquad (2.34)$$

$$q_{i,i}^{(i+4)} = (\lambda_i/\theta_i)[1 - g_i(\theta_i)] \qquad (i = 1, 2), \qquad (2.35)$$

$$q_{i,3-i}^{(i+2)} = 2[g_i(\theta_0) - g_i(\theta_i)] \qquad (i = 1, 2), \qquad (2.36)$$

$$q_{i,i+10}^{(i+2,i+6)} = (2\lambda_i/\theta_0)[1 - g_i(\theta_0)] - (2\lambda_i/\theta_i)[1 - g_i(\theta_i)]$$

$$(i = 1, 2), \qquad (2.37)$$

$$q_{i,i+12}^{(i+2,i+8)} = (2\lambda_{3-i}/\theta_0)[1 - g_i(\theta_0)] - (2\lambda_{3-i}/\theta_i)[1 - g_i(\theta_i)]$$

$$(i = 1, 2), \qquad (2.38)$$

$$q_{i+10,15-i}^{(11-i)} = (\lambda_i/\theta_0)[1 - g_{3-i}(\theta_0)] \qquad (i = 1, 2), \qquad (2.39)$$

$$q_{i+10,i} = g_{3-i}(\theta_0) \qquad (i = 1, 2), \qquad (2.40)$$

$$q_{i+12,3-i} = 1 \qquad (i = 1, 2). \qquad (2.41)$$

We obtain the limiting probabilities π_i $(i \in \underline{R}_3)$ for the embedded MC by solving the following equations:

$$\underline{\pi} = \underline{\pi} \cdot \underline{Q}_3 \quad \text{and} \quad \sum_{k \in \underline{R}_3} \pi_k = 1 , \qquad (2.42)$$

where

$$\underline{\pi} = [\pi_0, \pi_1, \pi_2, \pi_{11}, \pi_{12}, \pi_{13}, \pi_{14}]. \qquad (2.43)$$

The unconditional means μ_i $(i \in \underline{R}_3)$ neglecting the non-regeneration points are given by

$$\mu_0 = 1/2\theta_0, \qquad (2.44)$$

$$\mu_i = 1/\theta_i \qquad (i = 1, 2), \qquad (2.45)$$

$$\mu_{i+10} = 1/\theta_{3-i} \qquad (i = 1, 2), \qquad (2.46)$$

$$\mu_{i+12} = 1/\theta_{3-i} \qquad (i = 1, 2). \qquad (2.47)$$

We calculate the mean recurrence times ℓ_{ii}:

$$\ell_{ii} = \sum_{k \in \underline{R}_3} \pi_k \mu_k / \pi_i \qquad (i \in \underline{R}_3). \qquad (2.48)$$

The unconditional means ξ_i $(i \in \underline{A}_3)$ not neglecting the non-regeneration points are given by

$$\xi_0 = \mu_0 = 1/2\theta_0 , \qquad (2.49)$$

$$\xi_i = (1/\theta_i)[1 - g_i(\theta_i)] \qquad (i = 1, 2), \qquad (2.50)$$

$$\xi_{i+2} = (2/\theta_0)[1 - g_i(\theta_0)] - (2/\theta_i)[1 - g_i(\theta_i)]$$

$$\qquad (i = 1, 2), \qquad (2.51)$$

$$\xi_{i+10} = (1/\theta_0)[1 - g_{3-i}(\theta_0)] \qquad (i = 1, 2). \qquad (2.52)$$

From the above results we calculate the limiting probabilities p_i (i ϵ $\underline{A}_3$):

$$p_i = \xi_i/\ell_{ii} \qquad (i \epsilon \underline{A}_3 \cap \underline{R}_3, \text{i.e., } i = 0, 1, 2, 11, 12), \qquad (2.53)$$

$$p_i = \xi_i/\ell_{i-2,i-2} \qquad (i \epsilon \underline{A}_3 \cap \underline{NR}_3, \text{ i.e., } i = 3, 4). \qquad (2.54)$$

Thus, we obtain the limiting availability for the multi system:

$$A_3 = \sum_{k \epsilon \underline{A}_3} p_k . \qquad (2.55)$$

We further obtain the expected number of occurring the system break-down per unit of time in the steady-state:

$$F_3 = \sum_{k=1}^{2} [(q_{k,k+4} + q_{k,k+6}^{(k+2)} + q_{k,k+8}^{(k+2)})/\ell_{kk}$$

$$+ (q_{k+10,9-k} + q_{k+10,11-k})/\ell_{k+10,k+10} + 1/\ell_{k+12,k+12}],$$

$$(2.56)$$

where

$$q_{i,i+4} = q_{ii}^{(i+4)} \qquad\qquad (i = 1, 2), \qquad (2.57)$$

$$q_{i,i+6}^{(i+2)} = q_{i,i+10}^{(i+2,i+6)} \qquad\qquad (i = 1, 2), \qquad (2.58)$$

$$q_{i,i+8}^{(i+2)} = q_{i,i+12}^{(i+2,i+8)} \qquad\qquad (i = 1, 2), \qquad (2.59)$$

$$q_{i+10,9-i} = q_{i+10,13-i}^{(9-i)} \qquad\qquad (i = 1, 2), \qquad (2.60)$$

$$q_{i+10,11-i} = q_{i+10,15-i}^{(11-i)} \qquad\qquad (i = 1, 2). \qquad (2.61)$$

From the above results we obtain the MTBF for the multi system:

$$B_3 = A_3/F_3 . \qquad (2.62)$$

2.4. Numerical Examples

We illustrate the numerical examples of the limiting availabilities and the MTBF's for the simplex system (model 1), the duplex system (

model 2-a), the dual system (model 2-b), and the multi system (model 3), which are developed in the preceding sections. The limiting availabilities and the MTBF's can be computed by specifying all the distributions which are suitable for each system. Let us assume the repair time distributions common to each system. We assume the gamma repair time distributions with shape parameter 2:

$$G_i(t) = 1 - (1 + 2\gamma_i t) \exp(-2\gamma_i t) \qquad (i = 1, 2), \qquad (2.63)$$

where the means of these repair time distributions are $1/\gamma_i$ ($i = 1, 2$), respectively.

We first compute the limiting availability for each system. Fig. 2.8 shows the dependence of the mean repair time $1/\gamma_2$ for units B_i ($i = 1, 2$) on the limiting unavailability for each system in cases when the mean failure times $1/\lambda_1$ for units A_i ($i = 1, 2$) and $1/\lambda_2$ for units B_i ($i = 1, 2$) are 800 hrs. and 1,000 hrs., respectively, and 1,600 hrs. and 2,000 hrs., respectively, where the limiting unavailabilities are given by $1 - A_i$ ($i = 1, 2, 3$: A_i; the limiting availability for each system). From Fig. 2.8, we can show that the three fault-tolerant computer systems (i.e., the duplex, the dual, and the multi systems) have extremely high availability as compared with the fault-intolerant computer system (i.e., the simplex system). Again from Fig. 2.8, we can show that the dual system ($a = 1$ in model 2) is worse than the duplex system ($a = 0$ in model 2) and the multi system from the viewpoint of the availability, and that the duplex system is better than the multi system up to some repair time and after that time, to the contrary, the multi system is better than the duplex system from the viewpoint of the availability. Fig. 2.9 shows that the dependence of the mean repair time $1/\gamma_2$ on the limiting availabilities for the duplex system and the multi system. From Fig. 2.9 , we can understand the distinction between those systems more clearly. Fig. 2.10 shows the dependence of the proportion a (see model 2 in Section 2.2) on the limiting availability for the duplex system. From these results, we can understand that the duplex system is better than the multi system from the viewpoint of the availability only when the failure rate of the off-line sub-system is only a little as compared with that of the on-line sub-system.

We next compute the MTBF for each system. Fig. 2.11 shows the dependence of the mean repair time $1/\gamma_2$ for units B_i ($i = 1, 2$) on the MTBF for each system in two cases when the mean failure times $1/\lambda_1$ and $1/\lambda_2$ are 800 hrs. and 1,000 hrs., respectively, and 1,600 hrs. and

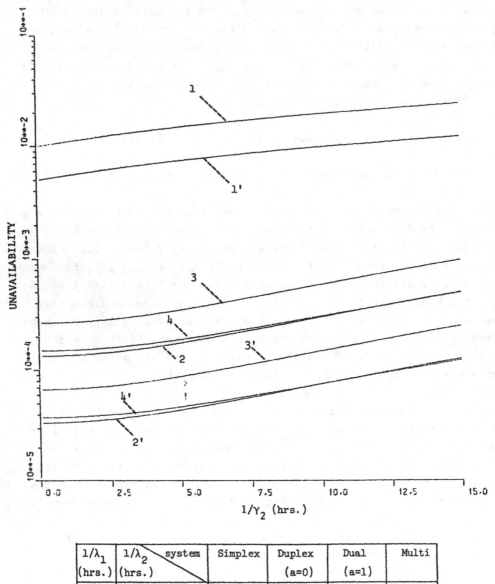

$1/\lambda_1$ (hrs.)	$1/\lambda_2$ (hrs.)	system	Simplex	Duplex (a=0)	Dual (a=1)	Multi
800	1,000		1	2	3	4
1,600	2,000		1'	2'	3'	4'

Fig. 2.8. The dependence of the mean repair time $1/\gamma_2$ on the limiting unavailability for each system, where $1/\gamma_1$ = 8 hrs.

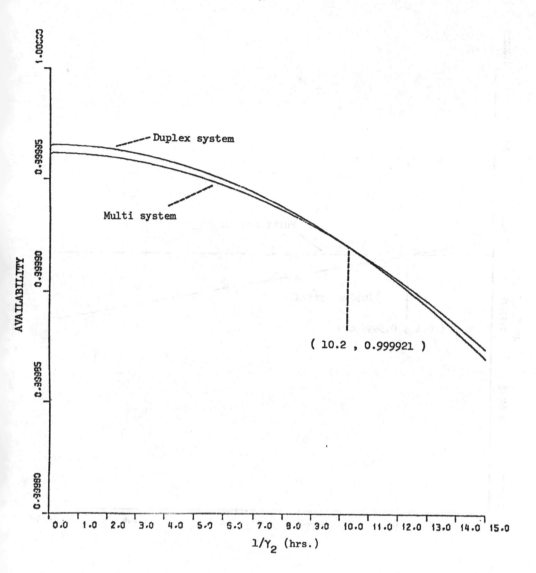

Fig. 2.9. The dependence of the mean repair time $1/\gamma_2$ on the limiting availabilities for the duplex system and the multi system, where $1/\lambda_1 = 1,600$ hrs., $1/\lambda_2 = 2,000$ hrs., $1/\gamma_1 = 8$ hrs., and $a = 0.001$.

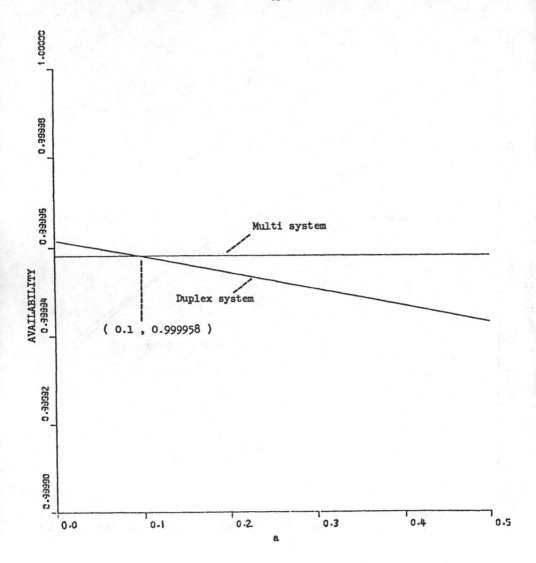

Fig. 2.10. The dependence of the proportion a on the limiting
availability for the duplex system, where $1/\lambda_1$ = 1,600 hrs., $1/\lambda_2$
= 2,000 hrs., $1/\gamma_1$ = 8 hrs., and $1/\gamma_2$ = 3 hrs.

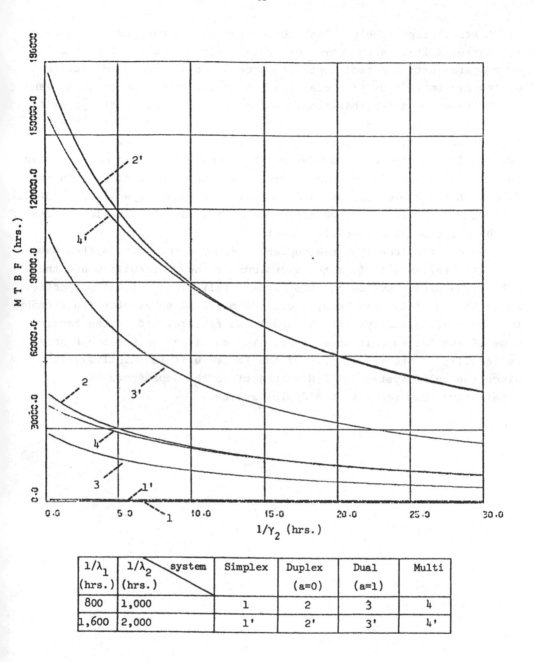

1/λ₁ (hrs.)	1/λ₂ (hrs.)	system	Simplex	Duplex (a=0)	Dual (a=1)	Multi
800	1,000		1	2	3	4
1,600	2,000		1'	2'	3'	4'

<u>Fig. 2.11.</u> The dependence of the mean repair time $1/\gamma_2$ on the MTBF
for each system, where $1/\gamma_1 = 8$ hrs.

2,000 hrs., respectively. From these results, we can understand that
the three fault-tolerant computer systems have extremely long MTBF's
as compared with the fault-intolerant computer system, and that the
duplex system (a = 0) is better than the multi system up to some mean
repair time and after that time, to the contrary, the multi system is
better than the duplex system from the viewpoint of the MTBF. These
results are the same as well as the results from the viewpoint of the
availability. However, the MTBF of the simplex system is never subject
to the dependence of the repair time. The mean repair time, when the
MTBF's of the duplex system and the multi system are specified identical
is longer than the mean repair time, when the limiting availabilities
of these systems are specified identical.

We can conclude that the duplex system and the multi system have
the ultra-reliability from the viewpoints of the availability and the
MTBF. The duplex system has the highest reliability if the proportion
a is only a little bit less, i.e., the off-line sub-system (in standby
for the on-line sub-system) has nearly no failure, and if the repair
time of the failed unit is shorter. The multi system has the highest
reliability if the repair time of the failed unit is relatively long
since the multi system is hardly subject to the dependence of the
repair time compared with the duplex system.

CHAPTER 3

COVERAGE-RELATED RELIABILITY ANALYSIS OF SOME COMPUTER ARCHITECTURES

3.1. Introduction

Some reliability evaluations of the typical ultra-reliable computer architectures with dynamic redundancy, i.e., a duplex system, a dual system, and a multi system, were discussed in Chapter 2.

In this chapter, we further consider the preceding three ultra-reliable systems (i.e., a duplex, a dual, and a multi systems) taking account of imperfect recovery and fault detection. That is, we introduce the concept of coverage (see Arnold (1973)), which is defined as a proportion of a fault from which a system automatically recovers. It is of great importance for the dynamic redundant computer systems to recover (re-configure) automatically if a fault is detected in any unit. In general, the ultra-reliable computer systems have the extremely important missions without interruption. Thus, we should avoid the occurrence of the system break-down for such computer systems as possible as we can. Hence, we have to consider the coverage-related models for evaluating more precisely the ultra-reliable computer systems. We also introduce a fault which cannot be detected by a monitor unit. A typical this kind of fault is a transient (intermittent) fault, e.g., the fault logic value is indeterminate when it varies between '0' and '1', but not in accord with design specifications, throughout the duration of the fault (see Avizienis (1976)). This kind of fault cannot be detected in the duplex system and the multi system, but can be detected in the dual system since the dual system is usually comparing and checking the outputs from both sub-systems.

We consider the coverage-related models composed of 4 units for the duplex system, the multi system, and the dual system, where we further consider the faults (which can be detected in the dual system) only for the dual system. Of our interest is to obtain both the limiting availability and the MTBF for each model by applying the unique modification of MRP's. Finally, numerical results of the limiting availability and the MTBF are presented and their comparisons are made for illustration.

3.2. Models

Assumptions

We have introduced some assumptions for the models of the simplex system, the duplex system, the dual system, and the multi system in Chapter 2. In addition to the assumptions (i) - (iv) in Section 2.2, we further introduce the following assumptions common to the models below unless otherwise specified:

(vi) The coverage is α_i in model i (i = 1, 2, 3), respectively.

(vii) When the unit A_i (i = 1 or 2) fails or recovers from the failure, and the automatic switchover cannot be performed, then the manual switchover time obeys the arbitrary distribution $M_{j1}(t)$ with mean $1/\delta_{j1}$ in model j (j = 1, 2, 3), respectively, and the unit B_i (i = 1 or 2) obeys the arbitrary manual switchover time distribution $M_{j2}(t)$ with mean $1/\delta_{j2}$ in model j (j = 1, 2, 3), respectively.

(viii) The time duration, when the undetected faults in the duplex and the multi systems (but the detected faults in the dual system) occur, obey the exponential time distributions with rates σ_1 and σ_2 for unit A_i (i = 1, 2) and unit B_i (i = 1, 2), respectively.

(ix) The repair times of the diagonostic times for the faults assumed in the assumption (viii) obey the arbitrary time distributions $G_{s_1}(t)$ and $G_{s_2}(t)$ with means $1/\gamma_{s_1}$ and $1/\gamma_{s_2}$ for units A_i (i = 1, 2) and B_i (i = 1, 2), respectively.

Notation

Introduce the following notations for analysis of the models below:

$\underline{U}_i$	; a set of all states in model i,
$\underline{R}_i$	; a set of regeneration points in model i,
$\underline{NR}_i$	; a set of non-regeneration points in model i,

$\underline{A}_i$; a set of operating states in model i,

$\underline{Q}_i$; limiting transition probability matrix composed of the possible regeneration points for model i,

A_i ; limiting availability for model i,

B_i ; MTBF for model i,

F_i ; the expected number of occurring the system break-down per unit of time in the steady-state for model i,

$Q_{ij}^{(k,\ell,m)}(t)$; the probability that after making a transition into state i, the process next makes a transition into state j via states k, ℓ, and m in an amount of time less than or equal to t,

$q_{ij}^{(k,\ell,m)}(s)$; LS transform of $Q_{ij}^{(k,\ell,m)}(t)$,

$g_{s_i}(s)$; LS transform of $G_{s_i}(t)$,

$q_{ij}^{(k,\ell,m)}$ $\equiv \lim\limits_{s \to 0} q_{ij}^{(k,\ell,m)}(s)$,

θ_a $\equiv \lambda_1 + \lambda_2 + a(\lambda_1 + \lambda_2)$,

θ_s $\equiv 2\lambda_1 + 2\lambda_2 + \sigma_1 + \sigma_2$,

θ_0 $\equiv \lambda_1 + \lambda_2$,

θ_1 $\equiv \lambda_1 + 2\lambda_2$,

θ_2 $\equiv 2\lambda_1 + \lambda_2$.

Model 1 (Duplex System)

Each pair of units A_i and B_i (i = 1, 2) forms a sub-system. One sub-system is used for on-line tasks and another sub-system is in standby for on-line. The standby sub-system usually executes off-line tasks. The on-line sub-system can perform its functioning when either sub-system functions. When a fault is detected in the on-line sub-system, the system behaves as follows; (1) automatic recovery (automatic switchover), i.e., the system recovers automatically by standby sub-system with probability (coverage) α_1, (2) manual recovery (manual switchover), i.e., the system recovers manually by standby sub-system with probability $\bar{\alpha}_1 \equiv 1 - \alpha_1$. For the two cases of recoveries above, the failed unit is repaired after the switchover. When a fault is detected in the off-line sub-system, the failed unit is immediately repaired since no switchover takes place.

From the above model, we introduce the following states (time instants) i (i ε U_1 = {0, 1, 2, 1', 2', 3, 4, 5, 6});

state   0; both sub-systems are operating,

state   1; when on-line unit A_i (i = 1 or 2) fails, system recovers
        automatically, otherwise off-line unit A_j (j $\neq$ i) fails,

state   2; when on-line unit B_i (i = 1 or 2) fails, system recovers
        automatically, otherwise off-line unit B_j (j $\neq$ i) fails,

state 1'; when on-line unit A_i (i = 1 or 2) fails, system recovers
        manually (system break-down),

state 2'; when on-line unit B_i (i = 1 or 2) fails, system recovers
        manually (system break-down),

state   3; unit A_i (i = 1 or 2) fails through state 1 (system
        break-down),

state   4; unit B_i (i = 1 or 2) fails through state 1 (system
        break-down),

state   5; unit A_i (i = 1 or 2) fails through state 2 (system
        break-down),

state   6; unit B_i (i = 1 or 2) fails through state 2 (system
        break-down),

where states i (i ε $\underline{R}_1$ = {0, 1, 2, 1', 2'}) are regeneration points and
states i (i ε $\underline{NR}_1$ = {3, 4, 5, 6}) are non-regeneration points. Then we can
show the state transition diagram among the states above in Fig. 3.1.

Model 2 (Multi System)

The system can perform its functioning in any combination of unit
A_i (i = 1, 2) and B_i (i = 1, 2) (i.e., units A_1 and B_1, units A_1 and
B_2, units A_2 and B_1, or units A_2 and B_2), and this system usually
requires all the units to execute on-line tasks. When a fault is detected at a unit, the failed unit is separated from the system and a
new system of the remaining units is performed by re-configuration.
After the repair is completed, the system including the unit restoring
is performed by re-configuration. Then the system re-configuration
is performed automatically with probability (coverage) α_2 and is performed manually with probability $\bar{\alpha}_2 \equiv 1 - \alpha_2$, where if the system
re-configuration is performed manually under the repair of a failed
unit, the repair is interrupted during the manual switchover time. If
two units A_i (i = 1, 2) or B_i (i = 1, 2) are under failure simultaneously, the system break-down takes place.

From the model above, we introduce the following states (time
instants) i (i ε $\underline{U}_2$ = {0, 1, 2, 1', 2', 1", 2", 3, 4, 3', 4', 3", 4",
5, 6, 7, 8, 9, 10, 11, 12, 13, 14});

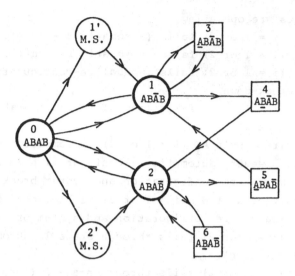

Fig. 3.1. State transition diagram of the coverage-related model of
the duplex system, where 'M.S.' represents the manual switchover,
' ◯ ' and ' ▢ ' represent states with regeneration point and non
-regeneration point, respectively, ' ◯ ' represents an operating
state, ' ‾ ' and '_' represent that the unit is under repair and the
unit is waiting for repair, respectively, and 'A' and 'B' represent
unit A_i (i = 1 or 2) and unit B_i (i = 1 or 2), respectively.

state 0; all units are operating,

state 1; unit A_i (i = 1 or 2) fails (automatic re-configuration),

state 2; unit B_i (i = 1 or 2) fails (automatic re-configuration),

state 1'; unit A_i (i = 1 or 2) fails (manual re-configuration and system break-down),

state 2'; unit B_i (i = 1 or 2) fails (manual re-configuration and system break-down),

state 1"; the repair of unit A_i (i = 1 or 2) is completed through state 1, however, automatic re-configuration is not performed (manual re-configuration and system break-down),

state 2"; the repair of unit B_i (i = 1 or 2) is completed through state 2 (manual re-configuration and system break-down),

state 3; unit B_i (i = 1 or 2) fails through state 1 (automatic re-configuration),

state 4; unit A_i (i = 1 or 2) fails through state 2 (automatic re-configuration),

state 3'; unit B_i (i = 1 or 2) fails through state 1 (manual re-configuration and system break-down),

state 4'; unit A_i (i = 1 or 2) fails through state 2 (manual re-configuration and system break-down),

state 3"; the repair of unit B_i (i = 1 or 2) is completed through state 4 or 11, however, automatic re-configuration is not performed (manual re-configuration and system break-down),

state 4"; the repair of unit A_i (i = 1 or 2) is completed through state 3 or 12 (manual re-configuration and system break-down),

state 5; unit A_i (i = 1 or 2) fails through state 1 (system break-down),

state 6; unit B_i (i = 1 or 2) fails through state 2 (system break-down),

state 7; unit A_i (i = 1 or 2) fails through state 3 (system break-down),

state 8; unit B_i (i = 1 or 2) fails through state 4 (system break-down),

state 9; unit B_i (i = 1 or 2) fails through state 3 (system break-down),

state 10; unit A_i (i = 1 or 2) fails through state 4 (system break-down),

state 11; the repair of unit A_i (i = 1 or 2) is completed through state 7,

state 12; the repair of unit B_i (i = 1 or 2) is completed through
state 8,

state 13; the repair of unit A_i (i = 1 or 2) is completed through
state 9,

state 14; the repair of unit B_i (i = 1 or 2) is completed through
state 10,

where states i (i ε $\underline{R}_2$ = {0, 1, 2, 1', 2', 1", 2", 3", 4", 11, 12, 13, 14}) are regeneration points and states i (i ε $\underline{NR}_2$ = {3, 4, 3', 4', 5, 6, 7, 8, 9, 10}) are non-regeneration points. Then, we can show the state transition diagram among the states above in Fig. 3.2.

Model 3 (Dual System)

Each pair of units A_i and B_i (i = 1, 2) forms a sub-system. Both sub-systems execute identical tasks, and the outputs of both sub-systems are always compared with checking units. When a fault is detected in either of the sub-systems, the failed sub-system is allowed to separate from the system and the remaining sub-system continues to execute on -line tasks, then the probability of automatic switchover (coverage) is α_3 and that of manual switchover is $\bar{\alpha}_3 \equiv 1 - \alpha_3$, and after the switchover the failed unit is repaired.

We assumed the exponential failure time distributions with rates λ_1 and λ_2 for units A_i (i = 1 , 2) and B_i (i = 1, 2), respectively, for the duplex and the multi systems. However, there are faults which cannot be detected with monitor units, e.g., transient (intermittent) faults which means fault logic value in the duplex and the multi systems, but can be detected in the dual system since the outputs of both the sub-systems are always compared with checking units. We assumed that these kinds of faults occurred with the exponential time distributions having rates σ_1 and σ_2 for units A_i (i = 1, 2) and units B_i (i = 1, 2), respectively (see the assumption (viii)). Other failures occur as same as the preceding models. The faults detected in all the systems are called the solid faults and the faults only detected in the dual system transient faults (see Avizienis (1976)).

From the model above, we introduce the following states (time instants) i (i ε $\underline{U}_3$ = {0, 1, 2, 1', 2', 1", 2", 1"', 2"', 3, 4, 3', 4', 5, 6, 5', 6'});

state 0   ; both sub-systems are operating,

state 1 [1"]   ; when a solid [transient] fault is detected in unit A_i (i = 1 or
               2), system recovers automatically (outputs are not coincident),

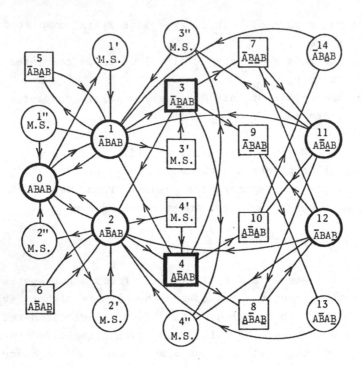

Fig. 3.2. State transition diagram of the coverage-related model of the multi system, where 'M.S.' represents the manual switchover, '◯' and '☐' represent states with regeneration point and non -regeneration point, respectively, '⬤' and '⬛' represent operating states, '‾' and '_' represent that the unit is under repair and the unit is waiting for repair, respectively, and 'A' and 'B' represent unit A_i (i = 1 or 2) and unit B_i (i = 1 or 2), respectively.

state 2 [2"]   ; when a solid [transient] fault is detected in
                 unit B_i (i = 1 or 2), system recovers automat-
                 ically (the outputs are not coincident),

state 1' [1"'] ; when a solid [transient] fault is detected in
                 unit A_i (i = 1 or 2), system recovers manually
                 (the outputs are not coincident and system break
                 -down),

state 2' [2"'] ; when a solid [transient] fault is detected in
                 unit B_i (i = 1 or 2), system recovers manually
                 (the outputs are not coincident and system break
                 -down),

state 3 [3']   ; a solid fault is detected in unit A_i (i = 1 or 2)
                 through state 1 [state 1"] (system break-down),

state 4 [4']   ; a solid fault is detected in unit B_i (i = 1 or 2)
                 through state 1 [state 1"] (system break-down),

state 5 [5']   ; a solid fault is detected in unit A_i (i = 1 or 2)
                 through state 2 [state 2"] (system break-down),

state 6 [6']   ; a solid fault is detected in unit B_i (i = 1 or 2)
                 through state 2 [state 2"] (system break-down),

where states i (i ϵ $\underline{R}_3$ = {0, 1, 2, 1', 2', 1", 2"}) are regeneration
points and states i (i ϵ $\underline{NR}_3$ = {3, 4, 3', 4', 5, 6, 5', 6'}) are non
-regeneration points. Then, we can show the state transition diagram
among the states above in Fig. 3.3.

3.3. Availability and MTBF

Model 1 (Duplex System)

Consider the model of the duplex system in Section 3.2. We first
derive the transition probabilities $Q_{ij}(t)$ (i ϵ $\underline{R}_1$, j ϵ $\underline{U}_1$), $Q_{ij}^{(k)}(t)$
(i ϵ $\underline{R}_1$, k ϵ $\underline{NR}_1$, j ϵ $\underline{U}_1$), and take the LS transforms for those,
respectively. Then we have

$$q_{0i}(s) = (\alpha_1 + a)\lambda_i/(s + \theta_a) \qquad (i = 1, 2), \qquad (3.1)$$

$$q_{0i'}(s) = \overline{\alpha}_1\lambda_i/(s + \theta_a) \qquad (i = 1, 2), \qquad (3.2)$$

$$q_{i0}(s) = g_i(s + \theta_0) \qquad (i = 1, 2), \qquad (3.3)$$

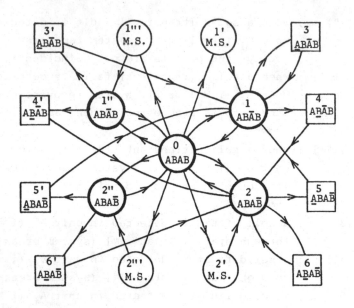

Fig. 3.3. State transition diagram of the coverage-related model of the dual system, where 'M.S.' represents the manual switchover, ' ◯ ' and ' ☐ ' represent states with regeneration point and non-regeneration point, respectively, ' ⬤ ' represents an operating state, ' ⁻ ' and '_' represent that the unit is under repair and the unit is waiting for repair, respectively, and 'A' and 'B' represent unit A_i (i = 1 or 2) and unit B_i (i = 1 or 2), respectively.

$$q_{i,j+2\times i}(s) = [\lambda_j/(s + \theta_0)][1 - g_i(s + \theta_0)] \quad (i, j = 1, 2), \quad (3.4)$$

$$q_{i',i}(s) = m_{1i}(s) \quad (i = 1, 2), \quad (3.5)$$

$$q_{ij}^{(j+2\times i)}(s) = [\lambda_j/(s + \theta_0)][g_i(s) - g_i(s + \theta_0)] \quad (i, j = 1, 2).$$

$$(3.6)$$

Using the results above and noting that states i (i ε $\underline{R}_1$) are regeneration points, we have the following limiting transition probability matrix for the embedded MC (see, e.g., Barlow and Proschan (1965)):

$$\underline{Q}_1 = \begin{pmatrix} 0 & q_{01} & q_{02} & q_{01'} & q_{02'} \\ q_{10} & q_{11}^{(3)} & q_{12}^{(4)} & 0 & 0 \\ q_{20} & q_{21}^{(5)} & q_{22}^{(6)} & 0 & 0 \\ 0 & q_{1'1} & 0 & 0 & 0 \\ 0 & 0 & q_{2'2} & 0 & 0 \end{pmatrix}, \quad (3.7)$$

where

$$q_{0i} = (\alpha_1 + a)\lambda_i/\theta_a \quad (i = 1, 2), \quad (3.8)$$

$$q_{0i'} = \bar{\alpha}_1\lambda_i/\theta_a \quad (i = 1, 2), \quad (3.9)$$

$$q_{ij}^{(j+2\times i)} = (\lambda_j/\theta_0)[1 - g_i(\theta_0)] \quad (i, j = 1, 2), \quad (3.10)$$

$$q_{i0} = g_i(\theta_0) \quad (i = 1, 2), \quad (3.11)$$

$$q_{i'i} = 1 \quad (i = 1, 2). \quad (3.12)$$

To obtain the mean recurrence times, we need the limiting probabilities and the unconditional means (see, e.g., Barlow and Proschan (1965)) for the embedded MC. We can obtain the limiting probabilities π_i (i ε $\underline{R}_1$) for the embedded MC by solving the following equations:

$$[\pi_0, \pi_1, \pi_2, \pi_{1'}, \pi_{2'}] = [\pi_0, \pi_1, \pi_2, \pi_{1'}, \pi_{2'}]\cdot\underline{Q}_1$$

and

$$\sum_{k \in \underline{R}_1} \pi_k = 1. \tag{3.13}$$

The unconditional means μ_i ($i \in \underline{R}_1$) neglecting the non-regeneration points are given by

$$\mu_0 = 1/\theta_a , \tag{3.14}$$

$$\mu_i = 1/\gamma_i \qquad\qquad (i = 1, 2), \tag{3.15}$$

$$\mu_{i'} = 1/\delta_{1i} \qquad\qquad (i = 1, 2). \tag{3.16}$$

Then we can calculate the **mean** recurrence times ℓ_{ii} ($i \in \underline{R}_i$):

$$\ell_{ii} = \sum_{k \in \underline{R}_1} \pi_k \mu_k / \pi_i \qquad\qquad (i \in \underline{R}_1). \tag{3.17}$$

The unconditional means ξ_i ($i \in \underline{A}_1$) not neglecting the non-regeneration points are given by

$$\xi_0 = \mu_0 = 1/\theta_a , \tag{3.18}$$

$$\xi_i = (1/\theta_0)[1 - g_i(\theta_0)] \qquad\qquad (i = 1, 2). \tag{3.19}$$

We can calculate the limiting probabilities p_i ($i \in \underline{A}_1$) for operating states:

$$p_i = \xi_i / \ell_{ii} \qquad\qquad (i \in \underline{A}_1), \tag{3.20}$$

and can easily obtain the limiting availability for the duplex system:

$$A_1 = \sum_{k \in \underline{A}_1} p_k . \tag{3.21}$$

We further obtain the expected number of occurring the system break-down per unit of time in the steady-state:

$$F_1 = \sum_{k=1}^{2} [(q_{k,1+2\times k} + q_{k,2+2\times k})/\ell_{kk} + 1/\ell_{k'k'}]. \tag{3.22}$$

From the results above we obtain the MTBF for the duplex system:

$$B_1 = A_1/F_1 .$$ (3.23)

Model 2 (Multi System)

Consider the limiting availability and the MTBF for model 2 (the multi system) in Section 3.2. We first derive the transition probabilities $Q_{ij}(t)$ ($i \in \underline{R}_2$, $j \in \underline{U}_2$), $Q_{ij}^{(k)}(t)$ ($i \in \underline{R}_2$, $k \in \underline{NR}_2$, $j \in \underline{U}_2$), $Q_{ij}^{(k,\ell)}(t)$ ($i \in \underline{R}_2$, $k,\ell \in \underline{NR}_2$, $j \in \underline{U}_2$), $Q_{ij}^{(k,\ell,m)}(t)$ ($i,j \in \underline{R}_2$, $k, \ell, m \in \underline{NR}_2$) and take the LS transforms for those, respectively. However, we omit the results here. From the results we obtain the limiting transition probability matrix $\underline{Q}_2$ for the embedded MC:

$\underline{Q}_2 =$

	(0)	(1)	(2)	(1')	(2')	(1")	(2")	(3")	(4")	(11)	(12)	(13)	(14)
	0	*	*	*	*	0	0	0	0	0	0	0	0
	*	*	*	0	0	*	0	0	*	*	0	*	0
	*	*	*	0	0	0	*	*	0	0	*	0	*
	0	*	0	0	0	0	0	0	0	0	0	0	0
	0	0	*	0	0	0	0	0	0	0	0	0	0
	*	0	0	0	0	0	0	0	0	0	0	0	0
	*	0	0	0	0	0	0	0	0	0	0	0	0
	0	*	0	0	0	0	0	0	0	0	0	0	0
	0	0	*	0	0	0	0	0	0	0	0	0	0
	0	*	0	0	0	0	0	*	0	0	*	0	*
	0	0	*	0	0	0	0	0	*	*	0	*	0
	0	0	*	0	0	0	0	0	0	0	0	0	0
	0	*	0	0	0	0	0	0	0	0	0	0	0

(3.24)

(See the next page in detail.)

(0)	(1)	(2)	(1')	(2')	(1")	(2")	(3")	(4")	(11)	(12)	(13)	(14)
0	q_{01}	q_{02}	$q_{01'}$	$q_{02'}$	0	0	0	0	0	0	0	0
q_{10}	$q_{11}^{(5)}$	$q_{12}^{(3)}+q_{12}^{(3;3)}$	0	0	$q_{11''}$	0	0	$q_{14''}^{(3)}+q_{14''}^{(3;3)}$	$q_{1,11}^{(3,7)}+q_{1,11}^{(3;3;7)}$	0	$q_{1,13}^{(3,9)}+q_{1,13}^{(3;3,9)}$	0
q_{20}	$q_{21}^{(4)}+q_{21}^{(4;4)}$	$q_{22}^{(6)}$	0	0	0	$q_{22''}$	$q_{23''}^{(4)}+q_{23''}^{(4;4)}$	0	0	$q_{2,12}^{(4,8)}+q_{2,12}^{(4;4,8)}$	0	$q_{2,14}^{(4,10)}+q_{2,14}^{(4;4,10)}$
0	$q_{1'1}$	0	0	0	0	0	0	0	0	0	0	0
0	0	$q_{2'2}$	0	0	0	0	0	0	0	0	0	0
$q_{1''0}$	0	0	0	0	0	0	0	0	0	0	0	0
$q_{2''0}$	0	0	0	0	0	0	0	0	0	0	0	0
0	$q_{3''1}$	0	0	0	0	0	0	0	0	0	0	0
0	0	$q_{4''2}$	0	0	0	0	0	0	0	0	0	0
0	$q_{11,1}$	0	0	0	0	0	$q_{11,3''}$	0	0	$q_{11,12}^{(8)}$	0	$q_{11,14}^{(10)}$
0	0	$q_{12,2}$	0	0	0	0	0	$q_{12,4''}$	$q_{12,11}^{(7)}$	0	$q_{12,13}^{(9)}$	0
0	0	$q_{13,2}$	0	0	0	0	0	0	0	0	0	0
0	$q_{14,1}$	0	0	0	0	0	0	0	0	0	0	0

$$= q'$$

The limiting transition probabilities are given by

$$q_{0i} = \alpha_2 \lambda_i / \theta_0 \qquad (i = 1, 2), \qquad (3.25)$$

$$q_{0i'} = \bar{\alpha}_2 \lambda_i / \theta_0 \qquad (i = 1, 2), \qquad (3.26)$$

$$q_{i0} = \alpha_2 \, g_i(\theta_i) \qquad (i = 1, 2), \qquad (3.27)$$

$$q_{ii''} = \bar{\alpha}_2 g_i(\theta_i) \qquad (i = 1, 2), \qquad (3.28)$$

$$q_{ii}^{(i+4)} = (\lambda_i / \theta_i) [1 - g_i(\theta_i)] \qquad (i = 1, 2), \qquad (3.29)$$

$$q_{i,3-i}^{(i+2)} = 2\alpha_2^2 [g_i(\theta_0) - g_i(\theta_i)] \qquad (i = 1, 2), \qquad (3.30)$$

$$q_{i,(5-i)''}^{(i+2)} = (\bar{\alpha}_2 / \alpha_2) q_{i,3-i}^{(i+2)} \qquad (i = 1, 2), \qquad (3.31)$$

$$q_{i,3-i}^{((i+2)\,;\,i+2)} = (\bar{\alpha}_2 / \alpha_2) q_{i,3-i}^{(i+2)} \qquad (i = 1, 2), \qquad (3.32)$$

$$q_{i,(5-i)''}^{((i+2)\,;\,i+2)} = (\bar{\alpha}_2 / \alpha_2)^2 q_{i,3-i}^{(i+2)} \qquad (i = 1, 2), \qquad (3.33)$$

$$q_{i,i+10}^{(i+2,i+6)} = 2\alpha_2 [(\lambda_i / \theta_0) [1 - g_i(\theta_0)] - (\lambda_i / \theta_i) [1 - g_i(\theta_i)]]$$
$$(i = 1, 2), \qquad (3.34)$$

$$q_{i,i+10}^{((i+2)\,;\,i+2,i+6)} = (\bar{\alpha}_2 / \alpha_2) q_{i,i+10}^{(i+2,i+6)} \qquad (i = 1, 2), \qquad (3.35)$$

$$q_{i,i+12}^{(i+2,i+8)} = 2\alpha_2 [(\lambda_{3-i} / \theta_0) [1 - g_i(\theta_0)] - (\lambda_{3-i} / \theta_i) [1 - g_i(\theta_i)]]$$
$$(i = 1, 2), \qquad (3.36)$$

$$q_{i,i+12}^{((i+2)\,;\,i+2,i+8)} = (\bar{\alpha}_2 / \alpha_2) q_{i,i+12}^{(i+2,i+8)} \qquad (i = 1, 2), \qquad (3.37)$$

$$q_{i'i} = 1 \qquad (i = 1, 2), \qquad (3.38)$$

$$q_{i''0} = 1 \qquad (i = 1, 2), \qquad (3.39)$$

$$q_{(5-i)'',3-i} = 1 \qquad (i = 1, 2), \qquad (3.40)$$

$$q_{i+10,i} = \alpha_2 g_{3-i}(\theta_0) \qquad (i = 1, 2), \qquad (3.41)$$

$$q_{i+10,(i+2)''} = (\bar{\alpha}_2 / \alpha_2) q_{i+10,i} \qquad (i = 1, 2), \qquad (3.42)$$

$$q_{i+10,15-i}^{(11-i)} = (\lambda_i/\theta_0)[1 - g_{3-i}(\theta_0)] \qquad (i = 1, 2), \qquad (3.43)$$

$$q_{i+10,13-i}^{(9-i)} = (\lambda_i/\theta_0)[1 - g_{3-i}(\theta_0)] \qquad (i = 1, 2), \qquad (3.44)$$

$$q_{i+12,3-i} = 1 \qquad (i = 1, 2). \qquad (3.45)$$

Solving the following equations:

$$[\pi_0, \pi_1, \pi_2, \pi_{1'}, \pi_{2'}, \pi_{1''}, \pi_{2''}, \pi_{3''}, \pi_{4''}, \pi_{11}, \pi_{12}, \pi_{13}, \pi_{14}]$$

$$= [\pi_0, \pi_1, \pi_2, \pi_{1'}, \pi_{2'}, \pi_{1''}, \pi_{2''}, \pi_{3''}, \pi_{4''}, \pi_{11}, \pi_{12}, \pi_{13}, \pi_{14}] \cdot \underline{Q}_2$$

and

$$\sum_{k \in \underline{R}_2} \pi_k = 1, \qquad (3.46)$$

we can obtain the limiting probabilities π_i ($i \in \underline{R}_2$) for the embedded MC. We obtain the following unconditional means μ_i ($i \in \underline{R}_2$) neglecting the non-regeneration points:

$$\mu_0 = 1/2\theta_0 , \qquad (3.47)$$

$$\mu_i = 1/\gamma_i + 2\bar{\alpha}_2 [\lambda_{3-i}/(\delta_{2,3-i}\theta_i)][1 - g_i(\theta_i)] \qquad (i = 1, 2), \qquad (3.48)$$

$$\mu_{i'} = 1/\delta_{2i} \qquad (i = 1, 2), \qquad (3.49)$$

$$\mu_{i''} = 1/\delta_{2i} \qquad (i = 1, 2), \qquad (3.50)$$

$$\mu_{(i+2)''} = 1/\delta_{2,3-i} \qquad (i = 1, 2), \qquad (3.51)$$

$$\mu_{i+10} = 1/\gamma_{3-i} \qquad (i = 1, 2), \qquad (3.52)$$

$$\mu_{i+12} = 1/\gamma_{3-i} \qquad (i = 1, 2). \qquad (3.53)$$

Then we calculate the mean recurrence times:

$$\ell_{ii} = \sum_{k \in \underline{R}_2} \pi_k \mu_k / \pi_i \qquad (i \in \underline{R}_2). \qquad (3.54)$$

The unconditional means ξ_i ($i \in \underline{A}_2$) not neglecting the non-regeneration points are given by

$$\xi_0 = \mu_0 , \tag{3.55}$$

$$\xi_i = (1/\theta_i)[1 - g_i(\theta_i)] \qquad (i = 1, 2), \tag{3.56}$$

$$\xi_{i+2} = 2[(1/\theta_0)[1 - g_i(\theta_0)] - (1/\theta_i)[1 - g_i(\theta_i)]]$$

$$(i = 1, 2), \tag{3.57}$$

$$\xi_{i+10} = (1/\theta_0)[1 - g_{3-i}(\theta_0)] \qquad (i = 1, 2). \tag{3.58}$$

We calculate the limiting probabilities for operating states:

$$P_i = \xi_i/\ell_{ii} \qquad (i \in \underline{A}_2 \cap \underline{R}_2 , \text{ i.e., } i = 0, 1, 2, 11, 12), \tag{3.59}$$

$$P_j = \xi_j/\ell_{j-2,j-2} \qquad (j \in \underline{A}_2 \cap \underline{NR}_2 , \text{ i.e., } j = 3, 4), \tag{3.60}$$

and using the results above, we can obtain the limiting availability for the multi system:

$$A_2 = \sum_{k \in \underline{A}_2} P_k . \tag{3.61}$$

We further obtain the expected number of occurring the system break-downs per unit of time in the steady-state:

$$F_2 = \sum_{k=1}^{2} [(q_{k,k+4} + q_{k,(k+2)'} + q_{k,k+6}^{(k+2)} + q_{k,k+8}^{((k+2)',k+2)} + q_{k,k+8}^{(k+2)}$$

$$+ q_{k,k+8}^{((k+2)',k+2)})/\ell_{kk} + 1/\ell_{k'k'} + 1/\ell_{k''k''} + 1/\ell_{(k+2)'',(k+2)''}$$

$$+ (q_{k+10,9-k} + q_{k+10,11-k})/\ell_{k+10,k+10} + 1/\ell_{k+12,k+12}] , \tag{3.62}$$

where

$$q_{i,i+4} = q_{ii}^{(i+4)} \qquad (i = 1, 2), \tag{3.63}$$

$$q_{i,(i+2)'} = 2\bar{\alpha}_2 (\lambda_{3-i}/\theta_i) [1 - g_i(\theta_i)] \qquad (i = 1, 2), \qquad (3.64)$$

$$q_{i,i+6}^{(i+2)} = q_{i,i+10}^{(i+2,i+6)} \qquad (i = 1, 2), \qquad (3.65)$$

$$q_{i,i+6}^{((i+2)',i+2)} = q_{i,i+10}^{((i+2)',i+2,i+6)} \qquad (i = 1, 2), \qquad (3.66)$$

$$q_{i,i+8}^{(i+2)} = q_{i,i+12}^{(i+2,i+8)} \qquad (i = 1, 2), \qquad (3.67)$$

$$q_{i,i+8}^{((i+2)',i+2)} = q_{i,i+12}^{((i+2)',i+2,i+8)} \qquad (i = 1, 2), \qquad (3.68)$$

$$q_{i+10,11-i} = q_{i+10,15-i}^{(11-i)} \qquad (i = 1, 2), \qquad (3.69)$$

$$q_{i+10,9-i} = q_{i+10,13-i}^{(9-i)} \qquad (i = 1, 2). \qquad (3.70)$$

From the results above, we can obtain the MTBF for the multi system:

$$B_2 = A_2/F_2 . \qquad (3.71)$$

Model 3 (Dual System)

Consider the limiting availability and the MTBF for the model 3 (the dual system) in Section 3.2. We can obtain the limiting transition probability matrix $\underline{Q}_3$ for the embedded MC similar to the preceding models:

$$\underline{Q}_3 = \begin{pmatrix}
0 & q_{01} & q_{02} & q_{01'} & q_{02'} & q_{01''} & q_{02''} & q_{01'''} & q_{02'''} \\
q_{10} & q_{11}^{(3)} & q_{12}^{(4)} & 0 & 0 & 0 & 0 & 0 & 0 \\
q_{20} & q_{21}^{(5)} & q_{22}^{(6)} & 0 & 0 & 0 & 0 & 0 & 0 \\
0 & q_{1'1} & 0 & 0 & 0 & 0 & 0 & 0 & 0 \\
0 & 0 & q_{2'2} & 0 & 0 & 0 & 0 & 0 & 0 \\
q_{1''0} & q_{1''1}^{(3')} & q_{1''2}^{(4')} & 0 & 0 & 0 & 0 & 0 & 0 \\
q_{2''0} & q_{2''1}^{(5')} & q_{2''2}^{(6')} & 0 & 0 & 0 & 0 & 0 & 0 \\
0 & 0 & 0 & 0 & 0 & q_{1'''1''} & 0 & 0 & 0 \\
0 & 0 & 0 & 0 & 0 & 0 & q_{2'''2''} & 0 & 0
\end{pmatrix} ,$$

$$(3.72)$$

where

$$q_{0i} = 2\alpha_3\lambda_i/\theta_s \qquad\qquad (i = 1, 2), \qquad (3.73)$$

$$q_{0i'} = 2\bar{\alpha}_3\lambda_i/\theta_s \qquad\qquad (i = 1, 2), \qquad (3.74)$$

$$q_{0i''} = 2\alpha_3\sigma_i/\theta_s \qquad\qquad (i = 1, 2), \qquad (3.75)$$

$$q_{0i'''} = 2\bar{\alpha}_3\sigma_i/\theta_s \qquad\qquad (i = 1, 2), \qquad (3.76)$$

$$q_{i0} = g_i(\theta_0) \qquad\qquad (i = 1, 2), \qquad (3.77)$$

$$q_{ij}^{(j+2\times i)} = (\lambda_j/\theta_0)[1 - g_i(\theta_0)] \qquad (i, j = 1, 2), \qquad (3.78)$$

$$q_{i'i} = 1 \qquad\qquad (i = 1, 2), \qquad (3.79)$$

$$q_{i''0} = g_{s_i}(\theta_0) \qquad\qquad (i = 1, 2), \qquad (3.80)$$

$$q_{i''j}^{(j+2\times i)'} = (\lambda_j/\theta_0)[1 - g_{s_i}(\theta_0)] \qquad (i, j = 1, 2), \qquad (3.81)$$

$$q_{i'''i''} = 1 \qquad\qquad (i = 1, 2). \qquad (3.82)$$

Note that q_{i0} $(i = 1, 2)$, $q_{ij}^{(j+2\times i)}$ $(i, j = 1, 2)$, and $q_{i'i}$ $(i = 1, 2)$ are the same as model 1 (see equations (3.11), (3. 10), and (3.12), respectively).

We solve the following equations:

$$[\pi_0 \quad \pi_1 \quad \pi_2 \quad \pi_{1'} \quad \pi_{2'} \quad \pi_{1''} \quad \pi_{2''} \quad \pi_{1'''} \quad \pi_{2'''}]$$

$$= [\pi_0 \quad \pi_1 \quad \pi_2 \quad \pi_{1'} \quad \pi_{2'} \quad \pi_{1''} \quad \pi_{2''} \quad \pi_{1'''} \quad \pi_{2'''}] \cdot \underline{Q}_3$$

and

$$\sum_{k \in \underline{R}_3} \pi_k = 1, \qquad\qquad (3.83)$$

and obtain the unconditional means μ_i $(i \in \underline{R}_3)$ neglecting the non-regeneration points:

$$\mu_0 = 1/\theta_s , \qquad\qquad (3.84)$$

$$\mu_i = 1/\gamma_i \qquad\qquad (i = 1, 2), \qquad (3.85)$$

$$\mu_{i''} = 1/\gamma_{s_i} \qquad\qquad (i = 1, 2), \qquad (3.86)$$

$$\mu_{i'} = \mu_{i'''} = 1/\delta_{3i} \qquad\qquad (i = 1, 2). \qquad (3.87)$$

Then we can calculate the mean recurrence times ℓ_{ii} $(i \in \underline{R}_3)$:

$$\ell_{ii} = \sum_{k \in \underline{R}_3} \pi_k \mu_k / \pi_i \qquad\qquad (i \in \underline{R}_3). \qquad (3.88)$$

Using the results above and obtaining the following unconditional means ξ_i $(i \in \underline{A}_3)$ not neglecting the non-regeneration points:

$$\xi_0 = \mu_0 , \qquad\qquad\qquad (3.89)$$

$$\xi_i = (1/\theta_0)[1 - g_i(\theta_0)] \qquad\qquad (i = 1, 2), \qquad (3.90)$$

$$\xi_{i''} = (1/\theta_0)[1 - g_{s_i}(\theta_0)] \qquad\qquad (i = 1, 2), \qquad (3.91)$$

we can calculate the limiting probabilities p_i $(i \in \underline{A}_3)$:

$$p_i = \xi_i / \ell_{ii} \qquad\qquad (i \in \underline{A}_3). \qquad (3.92)$$

Then, we can easily obtain the limiting availability:

$$A_3 = \sum_{k \in \underline{A}_3} p_k . \qquad\qquad (3.93)$$

We further obtain the expected number of occurring the system break-downs per unit of time in the steady-state:

$$F_3 = \sum_{k=1}^{2} [(q_{k,1+2\times k} + q_{k,2+2\times k})/\ell_{kk} + 1/\ell_{k'k'}$$

$$+ (q_{k'',(1+2\times k)'} + q_{k'',(2+2\times k)''})/\ell_{k''k''} + 1/\ell_{k''k'''}], \qquad (3.94)$$

where

$$q_{i,i+2\times i} = q_{i1}^{(1+2\times i)} \qquad\qquad (i = 1, 2), \qquad (3.95)$$

$$q_{i,2+2\times i} = q_{i2}^{(2+2\times i)} \qquad\qquad (i = 1, 2), \qquad (3.96)$$

$$q_{i", (1+2\times i)'} = q_{i"1}^{((1+2\times i)')} \qquad (i = 1, 2), \qquad (3.97)$$

$$q_{i", (2+2\times i)'} = q_{i"2}^{((2+2\times i)')} \qquad (i = 1, 2). \qquad (3.98)$$

From the results above, we obtain the MTBF for the dual system:

$$B_3 = A_3/F_3 . \qquad (3.99)$$

3.4. Numerical Examples

We show the numerical examples of the limiting availabilities and
the MTBF's for the duplex system (model 1), the multi system (model 2),
and the dual system (model 3), which are developed in the preceding
sections. The limiting availabilities and the MTBF's can be computed
by specifying all the parameters and by assuming the repair time distributions for each unit when the fault of the system is detected.
Let us consider the repair time distributions common to each system.
We assume the gamma repair time distributions with shape parameter 2
when the solid faults occur:

$$G_i(t) = 1 - (1 + 2\gamma_i t)\exp(-2\gamma_i t) \qquad (i = 1, 2), \qquad (3.100)$$

where the means of these repair time distributions are $1/\gamma_i$ $(i = 1, 2)$,
respectively, and the gamma repair time distributions with shape parameter 2 when the transient faults occur:

$$G_{s_i}(t) = 1 - (1 + 2\gamma_{s_i} t)\exp(-2\gamma_{s_i} t) \qquad (i = 1, 2), \qquad (3.101)$$

where the means of these repair time distributions are $1/\gamma_{s_i}$ $(i = 1,
2)$, respectively.

We first compute the limiting availability for each system. Fig.
3.4 shows the dependence of the coverage α_i $(i = 1, 2, 3)$ on the
limiting availability for each system in two cases when the mean
manual switchover times $1/\delta_{ij}$ $(i = 1, 2, 3; j = 1, 2)$ are 0.1 hrs.
and 1 hr., where we assume that $\alpha_1 = \alpha_2 = \alpha_3$ and $\delta_{11} = \delta_{12} = \delta_{21} =
\delta_{22} = \delta_{31} = \delta_{32}$. From these results we can understand that the
duplex system (a = 0) has the highest availability among the three
systems, and that the dual system has the higher availability than
the multi system up to some coverage, to the contrary, the multi system

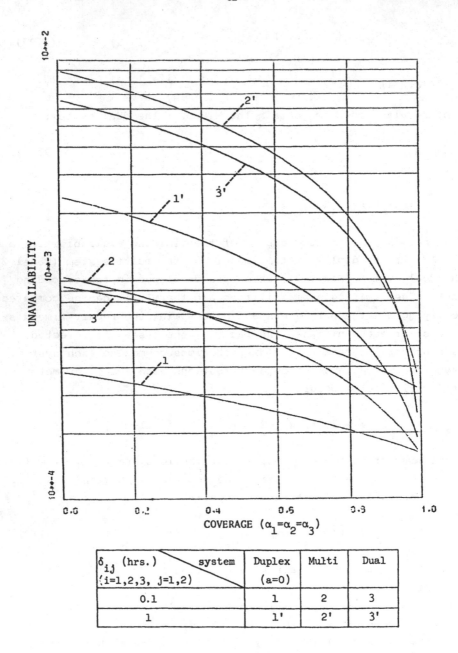

δ_{ij} (hrs.) system	Duplex (a=0)	Multi	Dual
(i=1,2,3, j=1,2)			
0.1	1	2	3
1	1'	2'	3'

__Fig. 3.4.__ The dependence of the coverage α_i (i = 1, 2, 3) on the limiting unavailability for each system, where $1/\lambda_1$ = 800 hrs., $1/\lambda_2$ = 1,000 hrs., $1/\gamma_1$ = 5 hrs., $1/\gamma_2$ = 8 hrs., $1/\sigma_1 = 1/\sigma_2$ = 2,000 hrs., and $1/\gamma_{s_1} = 1/\gamma_{s_2}$ = 0.1 hrs.

has the higher availability than the dual system after that coverage.

We next compute the MTBF for each system. Fig. 3.5. shows the dependence of the coverage α_i (i = 1, 2, 3) on the MTBF for each system, where $\alpha_1 = \alpha_2 = \alpha_3$. From these results we can understand that the duplex system has the longest MTBF among the three systems, and that the dual system has the longer MTBF than the multi system up to high coverage, but with considerably high coverage the multi system has the longer MTBF than the dual system.

In the figures above, we have computed the dependence of the coverage on the limiting unavailabilities and on the MTBF's under the assumption that all the coverages are equal. However, the coverage for each system might be different since the mechanism of the switchover are different for each system. It is actually difficult for the duplex system to make the standby sub-system such that the switchover is done automatically into the on-line if the on-line sub-system fails, since the standby sub-system is usually executing the off-line tasks, i.e., the mission of on-line tasks are different from that of off-line tasks. The on-line sub-system requires the special programs and the information files. The dual system executes the on-line tasks for using the two sub-systems, and both sub-systems execute identical tasks for the purpose of comparing the outputs. When either sub-system fails, the on-line system can continue its functioning only with the operating sub-system by separating the failed sub-system. Hence, the dual system might have the considerably high coverage. The multi system executes the on-line tasks for using all the units. When a unit failure is detected, the system can continue to operate with re-configuration without the failed unit. The mechanism of the re-configuration is very complex, but the automatic switchover (re-configuration) is able to succeed with advanced software and hardware techniques. Fig. 3.6 shows that the dependence of the coverage α_i (i = 1, 2, 3) on the MTBF for each system if the coverage is considerably high, and also shows the MTBF for the duplex system if the coverage $\alpha_1 = 0.5$. From these results and the facts that the mechanism of the switchover for each system is different, we can conclude that the dual system has the longest MTBF among the three systems except that the multi system has the considerably high coverage.

In Chapter 2, we have obtained the results that the dual system was the worst as compared with the duplex and the multi systems from the viewpoints of the availability and the MTBF. However, we have obtained the new results that the dual system can attempt to obtain the longest MTBF in the coverage-related models in this chapter.

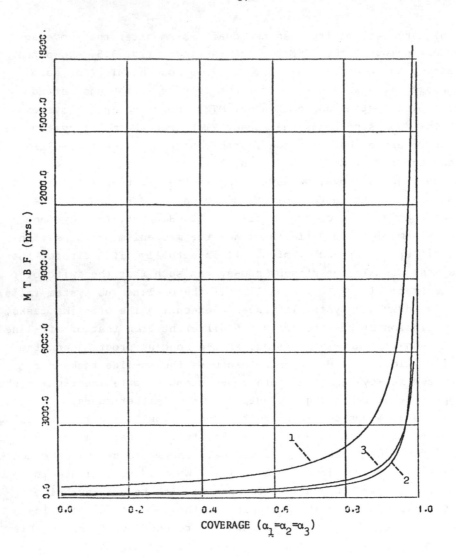

1: Duplex system (a = 0). 2: Multi system. 3: Dual system.

Fig. 3.5. The dependence of the coverage α_i (i = 1, 2, 3) on the MTBF for each system, where $1/\lambda_1$ = 800 hrs., $1/\lambda_2$ = 1,000 hrs., $1/\gamma_1$ = 5 hrs., $1/\gamma_2$ = 8 hrs., $1/\sigma_1 = 1/\sigma_2$ = 2,000 hrs., $1/\gamma_{s_1} = 1/\gamma_{s_2}$ = 0.1 hrs., and $1/\delta_{ij}$ = 0.1 hrs. (i = 1, 2, 3; j = 1, 2).

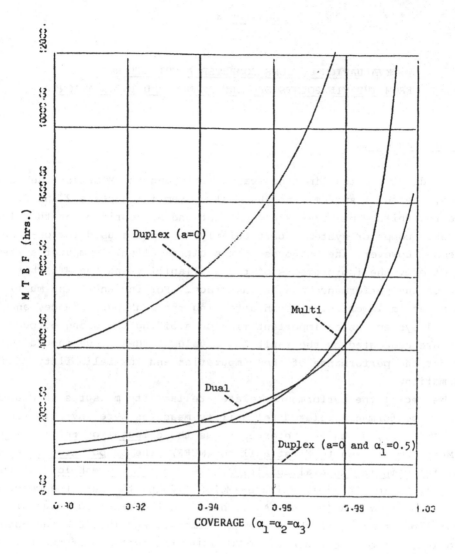

Fig. 3.6. The dependence of the coverage α_i (i = 1, 2, 3) on the MTBF for each system, where $1/\lambda_1$ = 800 hrs., $1/\lambda_2$ = 1,000 hrs., $1/\gamma_1$ = 5 hrs., $1/\gamma_2$ = 8 hrs., $1/\sigma_1 = 1/\sigma_2$ = 2,000 hrs., $1/\gamma_{s_1} = 1/\gamma_{s_2}$ = 0.1 hrs., and $1/\delta_{ij}$ = 0.1 hrs. (i = 1, 2, 3; j = 1, 2).

CHAPTER 4

EVALUATION OF SOME COMPUTER ARCHITECTURES
FROM THE VIEWPOINTS OF PERFORMANCE AND INFORMATION

4.1. Introduction

We discussed the limiting availability and the MTBF for the duplex
system, the multi system, and the dual system in Chapters 2 and 3.
These reliability measures are important and appropriate for the ultra
-reliable computer systems, particularly, which are used for on-line
systems. However, the purposes of the ultra-reliable computer systems
are not only the improvements of the availability and the MTBF but also
those of the performance and the accuracy. For instance, the multi
system has an important mission attaining the high performance, and
the dual system has an important mission avoiding the wrong outputs
which are generated by the fault logic values. Hence, we should
consider the performance of the computation and the reliability of the
information.

We recall the performance-related reliability measures in Chapter
1. Some performance-related reliability measures were investigated by
Beaudry (1978), which are referred to as the computation reliability,
the Mean Computation to First Failure (MCFF), the computation thresholds, the computation availabilities, the capacity threshold, and the
Mean Computation to First Failure (MCFF). In particular, the computation availabilities $A_c(t)$ and A_c , which are the expected value of the
computation capacity of the system at time t and in the steady-state
operation, are of great use for evaluating the system performance. We
shall consider the computation availability A_c in this chapter.

We next consider a reliability measure of the outputs. We introduce a new measure called the Information Unreliability Rate (IUR),
which is the expected number of generating the wrong outputs per unit
of time in the steady-state, where we assume that the wrong outputs
are generated by the transient faults (the undetected faults in the
duplex system and the multi system, see Chapter 3). Using the computation availability and the information unreliability rate, we shall
evaluate the ultra-reliable computer systems (i.e., the duplex, the

multi, and the dual systems) more precisely.

4.2. Computation Availability

Consider the computation availability A_c^i for each model i (i = 1, 2, 3)(i.e., a duplex system, a multi system, and a dual system). Recall that the (steady-state) computation availability is the expected value of the computation capacity of the system in the steady-state. Let c_k (k ε $\underline{A}_i$) denote the computation capacity of state k for model i (i = 1, 2, 3). Then the (steady-state) computation availability for model i is given by

$$A_c^i = \sum_{k \ \varepsilon \ \underline{A}_i} c_k p_k \qquad\qquad (i = 1, 2, 3), \qquad (4.1)$$

where $\underline{A}_i$ is a set of the operating state for model i and p_k is the limiting probability of the operating state k in model i, which was obtained in Chapter 3.

Duplex System

The computation availability of the duplex system is given by

$$A_c^1 = c_0 p_0 + c_1 p_1 + c_2 p_2 , \qquad\qquad (4.2)$$

where p_0 , p_1 , and p_2 are the limiting probabilities obtained in (3.20) in Section 3.3. Note that state 0 represents that both on-line and off-line sub-systems are functioning and states 1 and 2 represent that the on-line sub-system is functioning while the off-line sub-system is failed. Let ϕ_1 and ϕ_2 denote the computation capacities of the on-line and the off-line sub-systems, respectively. Then, the computation availability is rewritten by

$$A_c^1 = (\phi_1 + \phi_2)p_0 + \phi_1(p_1 + p_2). \qquad\qquad (4.3)$$

Multi System

The computation availability of the multi system is given by

$$A_c^2 = \sum_{k \in \underline{A}_2} c_k p_k \quad , \tag{4.4}$$

where $\underline{A}_2 = \{0, 1, 2, 3, 4, 11, 12\}$ and p_k ($k \in \underline{A}_2$) is the limiting probability obtained in (3.59) and (3.60) in Section 3.3. Recall the definitions of the states in Section 3.2. It is obvious from the definitions of the states that $c_4 = c_3$, $c_{11} = c_3$, and $c_{12} = c_3$. Then, we introduce ψ_1, ψ_2, ψ_3, and ψ_4 which represent the computation capacities when all the units are operating, unit A_i ($i = 1$ or 2) and units B_i ($i = 1$ and 2) are operating, units A_i ($i = 1$ and 2) and unit B_i ($i = 1$ or 2) are operating, and unit A_i ($i = 1$ or 2) and unit B_j ($j = 1$ or 2) are operating, respectively. Then, the computation availability is rewritten by

$$A_c^2 = \psi_1 p_0 + \psi_2 (p_1 + p_2) + \psi_3 (p_3 + p_4) + \psi_4 (p_{11} + p_{12}). \tag{4.5}$$

Dual System

The computation availability of the dual system is given by

$$A_c^3 = \sum_{k \in \underline{A}_3} c_k p_k \quad , \tag{4.6}$$

where $\underline{A}_3 = \{0, 1, 2, 1'', 2''\}$ and p_k ($k \in \underline{A}_3$) is the limiting probability obtained in (3.92) in Section 3.3. It is obvious from the definitions of the states in Section 3.2 that $c_2 = c_1$, $c_{1''} = c_1$, and $c_{2''} = c_1$. Let ω_1 denote the computation capacity when the system is operating. Then, we rewrite equation (4.6) as follows:

$$A_c^3 = \omega_1 (p_0 + p_1 + p_{1''} + p_2 + p_{2''}) \quad , \tag{4.7}$$

where we do not take account of any reliability of information since the dual system is usually comparing and checking the outputs from both sub-systems whenever they are functioning. We shall discuss the reliability of information in the next section.

4.3. Reliability of Information

Consider the information unreliability rate which is defined as the expected number of generating the wrong outputs per unit of time in the steady-state operation. In Chapter 3, we introduced the faults defined as the transient faults, which cannot be detected with monitor

units in the duplex system and the multi systems, but can be detected
in the dual system since the dual system is usually comparing and
checking the outputs from both sub-systems whenever they are functioning. The time durations, when the transient faults occur, obey the
exponential time distributions with rates σ_1 and σ_2 for unit A_i
(i = 1, 2) and unit B_i (i = 1, 2), respectively. Then, we assume that
the wrong output generates when the transient fault occurs. We have
the following possible cases of generating the wrong outputs;

> case 1; the duplex system is operating, then the undetected fault
>   rate is $\sigma_1 + \sigma_2$,
> case 2; the multi system is operating, then the undetected fault
>   rates are $2(\sigma_1 + \sigma_2)$, $2\sigma_1 + \sigma_2$, $\sigma_1 + 2\sigma_2$, and $\sigma_1 + \sigma_2$
>   if all the units, units A_i (i = 1 and 2) and unit B_i (i =
>   1 or 2), unit A_i (i = 1 or 2) and units B_i (i = 1 and 2),
>   and unit A_i (i = 1 or 2) and B_j (j = 1 or 2) are operating,
>   respectively.
> case 3; only one sub-system in the dual system is operating, then
>   the undetected fault rate is $\sigma_1 + \sigma_2$, i.e., if both the
>   sub-systems are operating, the system can detect the
>   wrong outputs.

We define the following Information Unreliability Rate IUR_1 for
the case 1,

$$IUR_1 = (\sigma_1 + \sigma_2) \sum_{k \varepsilon \underline{A}_1} p_k , \tag{4.8}$$

where p_k (k ε $\underline{A}_1$) is the limiting probability obtained in model 1
in Chapter 3 (see equation (3.20)). For the case 2,

$$IUR_2 = 2(\sigma_1 + \sigma_2) p_0 + (\sigma_1 + 2\sigma_2) p_1 + (2\sigma_1 + \sigma_2) p_2$$

$$+ (\sigma_1 + \sigma_2)(p_3 + p_4 + p_{11} + p_{12}) , \tag{4.9}$$

where p_i (i ε $\underline{A}_2$) is the limiting probability obtained in model 2 in
Chapter 3 (see equations (3.59) and (3.60)). For the case 3,

$$IUR_3 = (\sigma_1 + \sigma_2)(p_1 + p_2 + p_{1''} + p_{2''}) , \tag{4.10}$$

where p_i (i ε $\underline{A}_3$) is the limiting probability obtained in model 3 in

Chapter 3 (see equation (3.92)). From the results above, we can obtain
the information unreliability rate which is defined as the expected
number of generating the wrong outputs per unit of time in the steady
-state for each system.

4.4. Numerical Examples and Comparisons

We illustrate the numerical examples of the computation availabilities and the information unreliability rates for the duplex, the
multi, and the dual systems.

The computation availabilities can be computed on the basis of
the computation capacities and the limiting probabilities obtained in
Chapter 3. Recall the definitions in Section 4.2. Let ϕ_i (i = 1, 2), ψ_i
(i = 1, 2, 3, 4), and ω_1 denote the computation capacities for the
duplex, the multi, and the dual systems, respectively. In Chapter 2,
we considered a fault-intolerant computer system called the simplex
system. This system is basic for other fault-tolerant systems. We
assume that the computation capacity of the simplex system is 1 when
the system is operating. Then, we assume that the computation capacities ϕ_i (i = 1, 2), ψ_i (i = 1, 2, 3, 4), and ω_1 are proportional to
the computation capacity of the simplex system. We further introduce
the following proportional rates k_a, k_i (i = 1, 2, 3) for considering
the computation capacity for each system more easily, i.e., the computation capacity $\phi_2 = k_a\phi_1$ (0 < $k_a \le$ 1) for the duplex system, the
computation capacities $\psi_2 = k_1\psi_1$ (0 < $k_1 \le$ 1), $\psi_3 = k_2\psi_1$ (0 < $k_2 \le$ 1),
and $\psi_4 = k_3\psi_1$ (0 < $k_3 \le$ 1) for the multi system. These systems are
composed of four units, however, the computation capacity ω_1 of the
dual system, when all the units are operating, is less than or equal
to that of the simplex system composed of two units since both sub
-systems of the dual system execute identical tasks for the purpose
of comparing and checking the outputs, and the computation capacity
ψ_1 of the multi system, when all the units are operating, has not the
double computation capacity of the simplex system since the computation
capacity is degraded by the interaction of the units.

Fig. 4.1 shows the dependence of the proportional coefficient k_a
(i.e., the dependence of the computation capacity of the off-line system for the duplex system) on the computation availability for each
system. Fig. 4.2 shows the dependence of the computation capacity ψ_1
of the multi system, when all the units are operating, on the computation availability for each system. From the results above, we under-

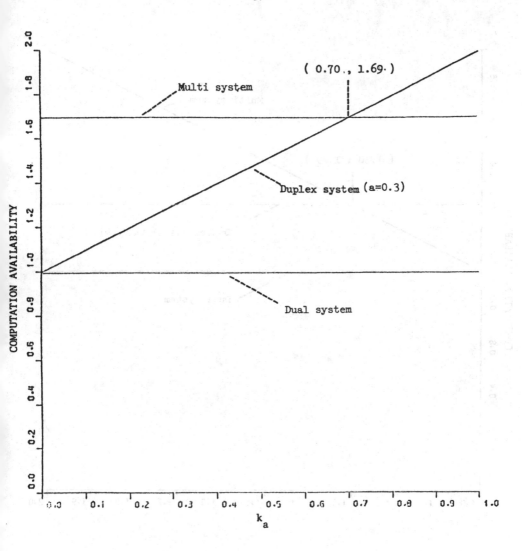

Fig. 4.1. The dependence of the proportion k_a on the computation availability for the duplex system, where $1/\lambda_1$ = 1,600 hrs., $1/\lambda_2$ = 2,000 hrs., $1/\gamma_1$ = 8 hrs., $1/\gamma_2$ = 3 hrs., $1/\sigma_1$ = $1/\sigma_2$ = 2,000 hrs., $1/\gamma_{s_1}$ = $1/\gamma_{s_2}$ = 0.1 hrs., α_i = 1 (i = 1, 2, 3), ϕ_1 = 1, ψ_1 = 1.7, k_1 = 0.7, k_2 = 0.8, k_3 = $1/\psi_1$, and ω_1 = 1.

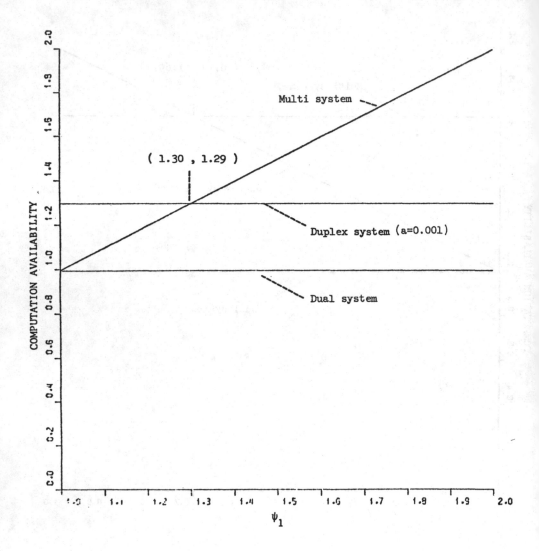

Fig. 4.2. The dependence of the capacity ψ_1 of the multi system on the computation availability for the multi system, where $1/\lambda_1$ = 1,600 hrs., $1/\lambda_2$ = 2,000 hrs., $1/\gamma_1$ = 8 hrs., $1/\gamma_2$ = 3 hrs., $1/\sigma_1 = 1/\sigma_2$ = 2,000 hrs., $1/\gamma_{s_1} = 1/\gamma_{s_2}$ = 0.1 hrs., α_i = 1 (i = 1, 2, 3), ϕ_1 = 1, k_a = 0.3, k_1 = 0.7, k_2 = 0.8, $k_3 = 1/\psi_1$, and ω_1 = 1.

stand that the multi system has the higher performance than the duplex
system under the reasonable conditions. To the contrary, the duplex
system has the possibility of attaining the high performance if the
off-line sub-system has the higher performance, e.g., a case that the
off-line sub-system is used for on-line tasks (note that, if the off
-line sub-system has the high performance, the reliability of the off
-line sub-system goes down).

The information unreliability rates can be computed on the basis
of the limiting probabilities obtained in Chapter 3 and the transient
fault rates introduced in Chapter 3. Fig. 4.3 shows the dependence
of the transient fault rates σ_1 and σ_2 on the information unreliability rate for each system. Table 4.1 shows the numerical examples
of the information unreliability rates for each system. From these
results, we understand that the dual system is extremely highly reliable from the viewpoint of information compared with other systems. We
further understand that the multi system is worse than the duplex
system from the viewpoint of the information unreliability rate, but
the distinction is a little bit less.

From all the results above, we can conclude that the multi system
has the highest performance and that the dual system has the highest
reliability of information among the three systems.

Table 4.1. The dependence of the mean transient faulty time on the
information unreliability rate for each system, where $1/\gamma_1$ = 5 hrs.,
$1/\gamma_2$ = 8 hrs., $1/\gamma_{s_1}$ = $1/\gamma_{s_2}$ = 0.1 hrs., α_1 = 0.5, α_2 = α_3 = 0.9, $1/\delta_{ij}$
= 1 hr. (i = 1, 2, 3; j = 1, 2), $1/\lambda_1$ = 800 hrs., and $1/\lambda_2$ = 1,000 hrs.

σ_i (i = 1, 2) (hrs.)	Information Unreliability Rate		
	Duplex (a=0)	Multi	Dual
10^2	0.0396675	0.0396739	0.0006269
$10^{2.5}$	0.0125439	0.0125460	0.0001830
10^3	0.0039667	0.0039674	0.0000562
$10^{3.5}$	0.0012544	0.0012546	0.0000176
10^4	0.0003966	0.0003967	0.0000055

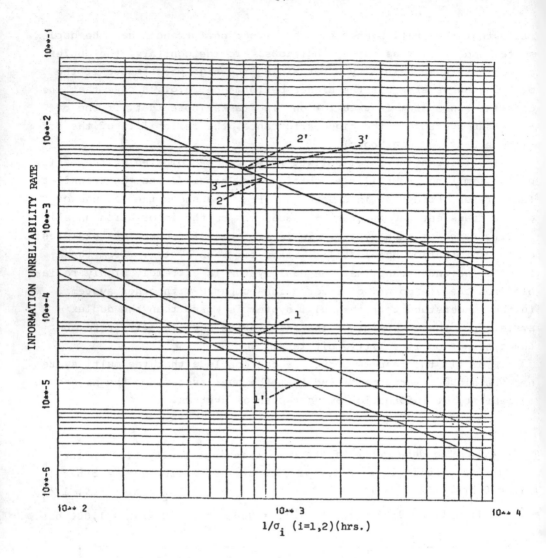

$1/\lambda_1$ (hrs.)	$1/\lambda_2$ (hrs.) system	Dual	Multi	Duplex (a=0)
800	1,000	1	2	3
1,600	2,000	1'	2'	3'

<u>Fig. 4.3.</u> The dependence of the mean transient faulty times $1/\sigma_i$ (i = 1, 2) on the information unreliability rate for each system, where $1/\gamma_1$ = 5 hrs., $1/\gamma_2$ = 8 hrs., $1/\gamma_{s_1} = 1/\gamma_{s_2}$ = 0.1 hrs., α_1 = 0.5, $\alpha_2 = \alpha_3$ = 0.9, $1/\delta_{ij}$ = 1 hr. (i = 1, 2, 3; j = 1, 2).

CHAPTER 5

RELIABILITY ANALYSIS OF THREE-UNIT HYBRID REDUNDANT SYSTEMS

5.1. Introduction

In Chapters 2, 3, and 4, we have discussed a duplex system, a
multi system, and a dual system from the viewpoints of the reliability
and the performance. In this chapter, we are interested in a three-unit
(-processor) hybrid redundant system which is composed of a two-unit
multi system and of a standby redundant (single) unit. Of course, the
standby redundant unit is used as the back-up system of the main multi
system. Such a three-unit hybrid redundant system is applied in the
real world to attain the high reliability and the high performance.
For instance, the so-called "HOPS" (Heart Online Processing System)
(see Abe (1977) and Abe et al. (1977)) by the Dai-Ichi Kangyo Bank,
LTD, one of the largest banks in Japan, is an on-line banking system
composed of three sets of FACOM 230-75's and Monitor VII program, which
is capable of executing approximately 300,000 transactions per hour,
per set.

In this chapter, we consider such a three-unit hybrid redundant
system and derive the reliability and the performance-related reliability measures which are defined in Chapter 1. In particular, we
compare such a three-unit hybrid redundant system with a two-unit multi
system, and show the improvements of the reliability and the performance
by introducing a standby redundant (single) unit. We further show the
dependence of the types of the repair time distributions on the availability, the MTBF, and the computation availability by assuming the
gamma distributions with shape parameter k, where k varies.

5.2. Models

In Chapters 2, 3, and 4, we have discussed models of 4 units,
where 2 units are the identical processing units and 2 units are the
identical storage units. In this chapter, we consider two models of

a two-unit multi system and a three-unit hybrid redundant system, where each unit is composed of a processing unit, a storage unit and the necessary peripherals. We introduce such two models for comparison. However, our aims are to analyze and evaluate the three-unit hybrid redundant system thoroughly. Introduce the following assumptions common to the models below unless otherwise specified:

(i) When two units can be functioning as the on-line, the failure law of the on-line two units obeys the bivariate exponential distribution (see Barlow and Proschan (1975), Chapter 5):

$$F(t_1, t_2) = 1 - e^{-(\lambda_1 + \lambda_{12})t_1} - e^{-(\lambda_1 + \lambda_{12})t_2}$$
$$- e^{-\lambda_1(t_1 + t_2) - \lambda_{12} \max(t_1, t_2)} . \qquad (5.1)$$

(ii) When only one unit can be functioning as the on-line, the failure law of the on-line unit obeys the exponential distribution:

$$F(t) = 1 - e^{-(\lambda_1 + \lambda_{12})t} , \qquad (5.2)$$

which is the marginal distribution of the bivariate exponential distribution above in (5.1).

(iii) Each failed unit obeys the arbitrary repair time distribution $G(t)$ with mean $1/\gamma \equiv \int_0^\infty \bar{G}(t)dt$, where $\bar{G}(t) \equiv 1 - G(t)$.

(iv) The repair facility is a single and the repair discipline is 'first come, first served.'

(v) Each switchover is perfect and instantaneous.

In particular, only for the model of the three-unit hybrid redundant system, we further assume the following:

(vi) The failure law of the off-line standby unit obeys the exponential distribution:

$$F(t) = 1 - e^{-\lambda_2 t} . \qquad (5.3)$$

Notation

Introduce the following notations for analysis of each model i (i = 1, 2):

$\underline{U}_i$; a set of all states for model i,

$\underline{R}_i$; a set of regeneration points for model i,

$\underline{NR}_i$; a set of non-regeneration points for model i,

$\underline{A}_i$; a set of operating states for model i,

g(s) ; Laplace-Stieltjes (LS) transform of G(t),

$\underline{Q}_i$; limiting transition probability matrix composed of the possible regeneration points for model i,

A_i ; limiting availability for model i,

B_i ; MTBF for model i,

F_i ; the expected number of occurring the system break-down per unit of time in the steady-state for model i,

$\Lambda \equiv 2\lambda_1 + \lambda_{12} + \lambda_2$,

$\theta_1 \equiv 2\lambda_1 + \lambda_{12}$,

$\theta_2 \equiv \lambda_1 + \lambda_{12}$,

$1/\gamma \equiv \int_0^\infty \bar{G}(t)\,dt$,

A_c^i ; computation availability for model i.

Model 1 (Two-Unit Multi System)

Consider a model of the two-unit multi system in Fig. 5.1. This system is introduced to compare with a three-unit hybrid redundant system (model 2). The two-unit multi system is used as the on-line tasks. The failure law of the operating two units obeys the bivariate exponential distribution in (5.1), which implies that the probability law of the simultaneous failure of the two units obeys the exponential distribution with rate λ_{12} and the probability law of the failure of one unit obeys the exponential distribution with rate $\lambda_1 + \lambda_{12}$ (see the details in Barlow and Proschan (1975), Chapter 5).

Introduce the following states (time instants) i (i ε U_1 = {0, 1, 2, 3});

state 0; both two units are operating,

state 1; one unit fails, then the failed unit is repaired immediately and the system is functioning with one unit,

state 2; both units fail simultaneously, then one of the failed

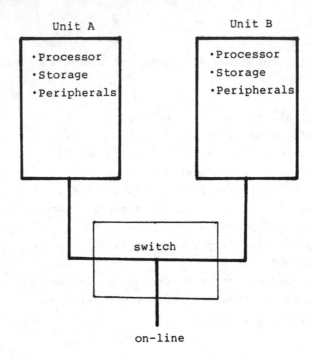

Fig. 5.1. A basic configuration of a two-unit multi system.

units is repaired immediately and the remaining unit
waits for repair (system break-down),

state 3; operating unit fails while the repair of the failed unit
is not completed (through state 1) (system break-down),

where states i (i ε $\underline{R}_1$ = {0, 1, 2}) are regeneration points and state
i (i ε $\underline{NR}_1$ = {3}) is a non-regeneration point. Then we can show the
state transition diagram among the states above in Fig. 5.2.

Model 2 (Three-Unit Hybrid Redundant System)

Consider a three-unit hybrid redundant system composed of two-unit
multi system and of a standby redundant unit (see Fig. 5.3). The two
-unit multi system is used as the on-line tasks and a standby unit is
used as the off-line tasks. Once one unit (or two units) of the on
-line sub-system fails (fail), the standby unit takes over its functioning and is reconfigured by the remaining two units (or one unit)
as the on-line sub-system. The system break-down takes place when all
three units fail simultaneously.

Introduce the following states (time instants) i (i ε $\underline{U}_2$ = {0,
1; 2, 3, 4, 5, 6, 7});

state 0; all units are operating,

state 1; one of the on-line two units fails, then the failed unit
is repaired immediately while the remaining two units
are reconfigured as the on-line sub-system,

state 2; the on-line two units fail simultaneously, then one of
the failed units is repaired immediately while the remaining failed unit waits for repair and the off-line
unit takes over the on-line operation immediately,

state 3; the off-line unit fails, then the failed unit is repaired immediately while the on-line two units are operating,

state 4; the repair is completed when all units are under failure,
then the repaired unit starts operation as the on-line
while one of the remaining failed units is repaired immediately and another of the remaining failed units
waits for repair,

state 5; one of the on-line two units fails while the repair of
the failed unit is not completed,

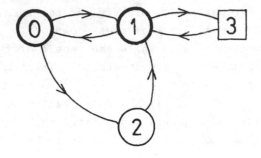

Fig. 5.2. State transition diagram among the states of the two-unit multi system, where '◯' and '▢' represent states with regeneration point and non-regeneration point, respectively, and '⬤' an operating state.

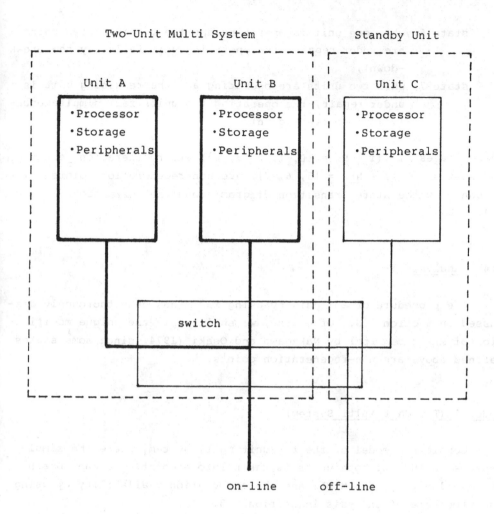

Fig. 5.3. A basic configuration of a three-unit hybrid redundant system.

state 6; when one unit is operating and the remaining two units
are under repair, the operating unit fails (system break
-down),

state 7; when two units are operating and the remaining unit is
under repair, the operating two units fail simultaneously (system break-down),

where states i (i ϵ $\underline{R}_2$ = {0, 1, 2, 3, 4}) are regeneration points
and states i (i ϵ $\underline{NR}_2$ = {5, 6, 7}) are non-regeneration points. Then
we can show the state transition diagram among the states above in Fig.
5.4.

5.4. Analysis

The procedure of analysis by using MRP's has been thoroughly discussed in Section 2.3. Of course, we shall apply the unique modification of MRP's developed by Nakagawa and Osaki (1974) since some states
defined above are non-regeneration points.

Model 1 (Two-Unit Multi System)

Consider a model of the two-unit multi system, where the simultaneous failure of both units is taken into account. We can obtain
the availability, the MTBF, and the computation availability by using
the procedure of analysis in Section 2.3.

We derive the transition probabilities $Q_{ij}(t)$ (i ϵ $\underline{R}_1$, j ϵ $\underline{U}_1$)
and $Q_{ij}^{(k)}(t)$ (i ϵ $\underline{R}_1$, k ϵ $\underline{NR}_1$, j ϵ $\underline{U}_1$), and take the LS transforms
for those:

$$q_{01}(s) = 2\lambda_1/(s + \theta_1) , \qquad\qquad (5.4)$$

$$q_{02}(s) = \lambda_{12}/(s + \theta_1) , \qquad\qquad (5.5)$$

$$q_{10}(s) = g(s+\theta_2) , \qquad\qquad (5.6)$$

$$q_{21}(s) = g(s) , \qquad\qquad (5.7)$$

$$q_{13}(s) = \theta_2[1 - g(s+\theta_2)]/(s + \theta_2) , \qquad\qquad (5.8)$$

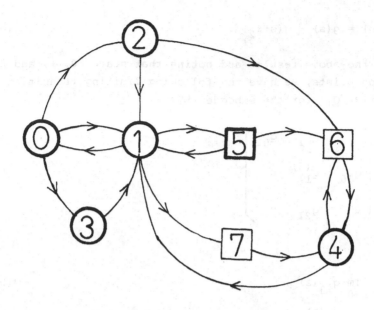

Fig. 5.4. State transition diagram among the states of the three-unit hybrid redundant system, where '◯' and '▢' represent states with regeneration point and non-regeneration point, respectively, and '●' and '■' operating states.

$$q_{11}^{(3)}(s) = g(s) - g(s+\theta_2) . \tag{5.9}$$

Using the above results and noting that states 0, 1, and 2 are regeneration points, we have the following limiting transition probability matrix $\underline{Q}_1$ for the embedded MC:

$$\underline{Q}_1 = \begin{pmatrix} 0 & q_{01} & q_{02} \\ q_{10} & q_{11}^{(3)} & 0 \\ 0 & q_{21} & 0 \end{pmatrix} , \tag{5.10}$$

where

$$q_{ij} \equiv \lim_{s\to 0} q_{ij}(s) , \tag{5.11}$$

$$q_{ij}^{(k)} \equiv \lim_{s\to 0} q_{ij}^{(k)}(s) . \tag{5.12}$$

Solving the following equations:

$$[\pi_0 , \pi_1 , \pi_2] = [\pi_0 , \pi_1 , \pi_2]\cdot\underline{Q}_2 \quad \text{and} \quad \sum_{k=0}^{2} \pi_k = 1 , \tag{5.13}$$

we can obtain the limiting probabilities π_i ($i \in \underline{R}_1$) for the embedded MC. The unconditional means μ_i ($i \in \underline{R}_1$) neglecting the non-regeneration point are given by

$$\mu_0 = 1/\theta_1 , \tag{5.14}$$

$$\mu_1 = \mu_2 = 1/\gamma . \tag{5.15}$$

Then we can calculate the mean recurrence times:

$$\ell_{ii} = \sum_{k \in \underline{R}_1} \pi_k \mu_k / \pi_i \quad (i \in \underline{R}_1). \tag{5.16}$$

The unconditional means ξ_i ($i \in \underline{A}_1$) not neglecting the non-regeneration point are given by

$$\xi_0 = \mu_0 , \tag{5.17}$$

$$\xi_1 = [1 - g(\theta_2)]/\theta_2 \ . \tag{5.18}$$

From the above results we calculate the limiting probabilities for operating states :

$$P_i = \xi_i / \ell_{ii} \qquad\qquad (i = 0, 1). \tag{5.19}$$

Thus, we obtain the limiting availability:

$$A_1 = P_0 + P_1 \ . \tag{5.20}$$

We further obtain the expected number of occurring the system break -down per unit of time in the steady-state:

$$F_1 = q_{02}/\ell_{00} + q_{13}/\ell_{11} \ . \tag{5.21}$$

From the above results we obtain the MTBF:

$$B_1 = A_1/F_1 \ . \tag{5.22}$$

We finally obtain the computation availability:

$$A_c^1 = c_0 P_0 + c_1 P_1 \ , \tag{5.23}$$

where P_0 and P_1 are obtained in (5.19), and c_0 and c_1 are the computation capacities for states 0 and 1, respectively. We specify the computation capacities c_0 and c_1 in the numerical examples of the next section.

Model 2 (Three-Unit Hybrid Redundant System)

We just give the LS transforms $q_{ij}(s)$ ($i \in \underline{R}_2$, $j \in \underline{U}_2$), $q_{ij}^{(k)}(s)$ ($i \in \underline{R}_2$, $k \in \underline{NR}_2$, $j \in \underline{U}_2$), and $q_{ij}^{(k,\ell)}(s)$ ($i \in \underline{R}_2$, $k, \ell \in \underline{NR}_2$, $j \in \underline{U}_2$):

$$q_{01}(s) = 2\lambda_1/(s + \Lambda) \ , \tag{5.24}$$

$$q_{02}(s) = \lambda_{12}/(s + \Lambda) \ , \tag{5.25}$$

$$q_{03}(s) = \lambda_2/(s + \Lambda) \quad , \tag{5.26}$$

$$q_{10}(s) = g(s+\theta_1) \quad , \tag{5.27}$$

$$q_{15}(s) = 2\lambda_1[1 - g(s+\theta_1)]/(s + \theta_1) \quad , \tag{5.28}$$

$$q_{17}(s) = \lambda_{12}[1 - g(s+\theta_1)]/(s + \theta_1) \quad , \tag{5.29}$$

$$q_{11}^{(5)}(s) = 2[g(s+\theta_2) - g(s+\theta_1)] \quad , \tag{5.30}$$

$$q_{16}^{(5)}(s) = 2\theta_2\{[1 - g(s+\theta_2)]/(s + \theta_2) - [1 - g(s+\theta_1)]/(s + \theta_1)\} \quad , \tag{5.31}$$

$$q_{14}^{(5,6)}(s) = (2\lambda_1/\theta_1)[g(s) - \theta_1 g(s+\theta_2)/\lambda_1 + \theta_2 g(s+\theta_1)/\lambda_1] \quad , \tag{5.32}$$

$$q_{14}^{(7)}(s) = \lambda_{12}[g(s) - g(s+\theta_1)]/\theta_1 \quad , \tag{5.33}$$

$$q_{21}(s) = g(s+\theta_2) \quad , \tag{5.34}$$

$$q_{26}(s) = \theta_2[1 - g(s+\theta_2)]/(s + \theta_2) \quad , \tag{5.35}$$

$$q_{24}^{(6)}(s) = g(s) - g(s+\theta_2) \quad , \tag{5.36}$$

$$q_{31}(s) = 1 \quad , \tag{5.37}$$

$$q_{41}(s) = g(s+\theta_2) \quad , \tag{5.38}$$

$$q_{46}(s) = \theta_2[1 - g(s+\theta_2)]/(s + \theta_2) \quad , \tag{5.39}$$

$$q_{44}^{(6)}(s) = g(s) - g(s+\theta_2) \quad . \tag{5.40}$$

Using the above results and noting that states 0, 1, 2, 3, and 4 are regeneration points, we have the following limiting transition probability matrix $\underline{Q}_2$ for the embedded MC:

$$\underline{Q}_2 = \begin{pmatrix} 0 & q_{01} & q_{02} & q_{03} & 0 \\ q_{10} & q_{11}^{(5)} & 0 & 0 & q_{14}^{(5,6)}+q_{14}^{(7)} \\ 0 & q_{21} & 0 & 0 & q_{24}^{(6)} \\ 0 & q_{31} & 0 & 0 & 0 \\ 0 & q_{41} & 0 & 0 & q_{44}^{(6)} \end{pmatrix} \quad , \tag{5.41}$$

where

$$q_{ij} \equiv \lim_{s \to 0} q_{ij}(s) \quad , \tag{5.42}$$

$$q_{ij}^{(k)} \equiv \lim_{s \to 0} q_{ij}^{(k)}(s) \quad , \tag{5.43}$$

$$q_{ij}^{(k,\ell)} \equiv \lim_{s \to 0} q_{ij}^{(k,\ell)}(s) \quad . \tag{5.44}$$

Solving the following equations:

$$\underline{\pi} = \underline{\pi} \cdot \underline{Q}_2 \quad \text{and} \quad \sum_{k=0}^{4} \pi_k = 1 \quad , \tag{5.45}$$

where $\underline{\pi} = [\pi_0, \pi_1, \pi_2, \pi_3, \pi_4]$, we have the limiting probabilities π_i ($i \in \underline{R}_2$) for the embedded MC. The unconditional means μ_i ($i \in \underline{R}_2$) neglecting the non-regeneration points are given by

$$\mu_0 = 1/\Lambda \quad , \tag{5.46}$$

$$\mu_1 = \mu_2 = \mu_4 = 1/\gamma \quad , \tag{5.47}$$

$$\mu_3 = 0 \quad . \tag{5.48}$$

Then we can calculate the mean recurrence times:

$$\ell_{ii} = \sum_{k \in \underline{R}_2} \pi_k \mu_k / \pi_i \qquad (i \in \underline{R}_2) . \tag{5.49}$$

The unconditional means ξ_i ($i \in \underline{A}_2$) not neglecting the non-regeneration points are given by

$$\xi_0 = \mu_0 \quad , \tag{5.50}$$

$$\xi_1 = [1 - g(\theta_1)]/\theta_1 \quad , \tag{5.51}$$

$$\xi_2 = \xi_4 = [1 - g(\theta_2)]/\theta_2 \quad , \tag{5.52}$$

$$\xi_3 = \mu_3 \quad , \tag{5.53}$$

$$\xi_5 = 2[1 - g(\theta_2)]/\theta_2 - 2[1 - g(\theta_1)]/\theta_1 \quad . \tag{5.54}$$

From the above results we calculate the limiting probabilities for operating states:

$$p_i = \xi_i/\ell_{ii} \qquad\qquad (i = 0, 1, 2, 3, 4) \quad , \tag{5.55}$$

$$p_5 = \xi_5/\ell_{11} \quad . \tag{5.56}$$

The limiting availability is given by

$$A_2 = \sum_{k=0}^{5} p_k \quad . \tag{5.57}$$

We further obtain the expected number of occurring the system break-down per unit of time in the steady-state:

$$F_2 = (q_{16}^{(5)} + q_{17})/\ell_{11} + q_{26}/\ell_{22} + q_{46}/\ell_{44} \quad . \tag{5.58}$$

From the above results we obtain the MTBF:

$$B_2 = A_2/F_2 \quad . \tag{5.59}$$

We just give the computation availability:

$$A_c^2 = \sum_{i=0}^{5} c_i p_i \quad , \tag{5.60}$$

where p_i (i = 0, 1, 2, 3, 4, 5) are obtained in (5.55) and (5.56), and c_i (i = 0 , 1, 2, 3, 4, 5) are the computation capacities for state i, respectively. We specify all the computation capacities in the numerical examples of the next section.

5.4. Numerical Examples

Let us consider the numerical examples of the above results. Recall that our aims are to compare the two-unit multi system with the

three-unit hybrid redundant system. That is, we shall show how the
reliability and the performance are improved by introducing a standby
unit to the two-unit multi system (i.e., the three-unit hybrid redundant system).

We first specify all the parameters for each model. The failure
laws of the on-line and the off-line sub-systems are given by (5.1)
and (5.3), respectively, where the parameters are the constant failure
rates λ_1 , λ_{12} , and λ_2. It is natural to assume $\lambda_1 > \lambda_2$ since the
on-line failure rate λ_1 is greater than the off-line failure rate
λ_2. It is also noted that the constant failure rate λ_{12} is relatively small compared with the failure rates λ_1 and λ_2 since it represents the simultaneous failure rate of both units.

We next specify the repair law of the failed unit. It is generally assumed that the repair law obeys the non-exponential distribution
with a unimodal density such as the logarithmic normal distribution.
However, we assume a gamma (or Erlang) distribution with shape parameter k:

$$G(t) = \int_0^t \frac{(\mu k)^k x^{k-1} e^{-\mu kx}}{(k-1)!} \, dx = 1 - \sum_{i=0}^{k-1} \frac{(\mu kt)^i}{i!} e^{-\mu kt} \quad , \quad (5.61)$$

where the mean repair time is $1/\mu$. The gamma distribution in (5.61) includes some interesting distribution as k varies. For instance,
k = 1 implies an exponential distribution, and k→∞ implies a unit
step function (i.e., a degenerate distribution) at $1/\mu$. Fig. 5.5
shows the curves of the gamma density function:

$$dG(t)/dt = (\mu k)^k t^{k-1} e^{-\mu kt} / (k-1)! \quad , \quad (5.62)$$

where k = 1, 2, 3, 5, and 10. We see from Fig. 5.5 that these densi-
ties are unimodal when k > 1 (of course, we can verify this fact analytically).

Consider the unavailabilities of the two-unit multi system and the
three-unit hybrid redundant system, where the unavailability is defined
by making one minus the availability. We assume that $1/\lambda_1$ = 150 hrs.,
$1/\lambda_{12}$ = 1,000 hrs., $1/\lambda_2$ = 250 hrs., and the mean repair time $1/\mu$
varies from 0 hr. to 12 hrs. Fig. 5.6 shows the dependence of the
mean repair time $1/\mu$ on the unavailability for each system. For
instance, the decrease of the unavailability (i.e., the increase of
the availability) is from 0.009 (0.991) to 0.0013 (0.9987) by
introducing a standby unit to the two-unit multi system, where $1/\mu$ =

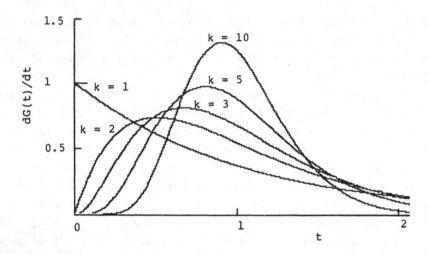

Fig. 5.5. The probability density function of the gamma (or Erlang) distribution when $1/\mu = 1$ and $k = 1, 2, 3, 5, 10$.

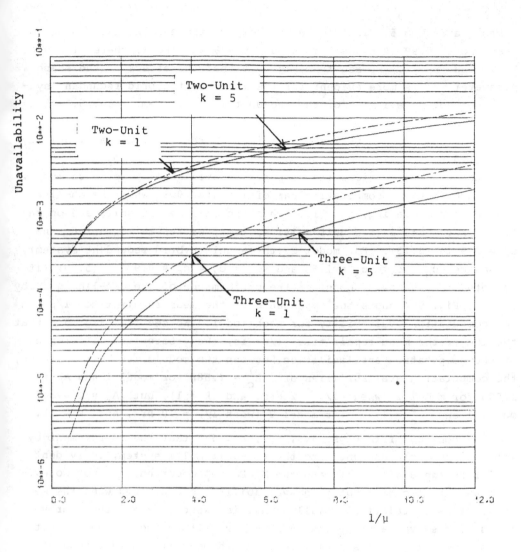

Fig. 5.6. The dependence of the mean repair time $1/\mu$ on the unavailability for each system, where $k = 1, 5$; $1/\lambda_1 = 150$ hrs., $1/\lambda_{12} = 1,000$ hrs., and $1/\lambda_2 = 250$ hrs.

6 hrs. and k = 5. That is, we can expect the availability going up
from about 0.99 (2 nines) to about 0.999 (3 nines), where $1/\mu = 6$
hrs. and k = 5. We see from Fig. 5.6 that the effect of the shape
parameter k is more evident for the three-unit hybrid redundant system, but not so evident for the two-unit multi system. Fig. 5.7 shows
the dependence of the mean repair time $1/\mu$ on the MTBF for each system. The tendency of the MTBF is similar to that of the unavailability
in Fig. 5.6.

Let us next consider the computation availability for each model.
We assume that the computation capacities are 0.9 when the on-line
one unit is operating, and 1.6 when the on-line two units are operating. For model 1 (two-unit multi system), we assume $c_0 = 1.6$ and
$c_1 = 0.9$ in (5.23). For model 2 (three-unit hybrid redundant system),
we assume $c_0 = c_1 = c_3 = 1.6$ and $c_2 = c_4 = c_5 = 0.9$ in (5.60) (it
is noted that we never consider the performance of the off-line standby
unit). Fig. 5.8 shows the dependence of the mean repair time $1/\mu$ on
the computation availability for each model. We see from Fig. 5.8 that
the longer the mean repair time $1/\mu$ is, the greater the difference
of the computation availabilities between two models is. For instance,
the computation availabilities are $A_C^1 = 1.580$ for model 1 and $A_C^2 =$
1.595 for model 2 (when $1/\mu = 2$ hrs. and k = 1), but $A_C^1 = 1.478$ for
model 1 and $A_C^2 = 1.573$ for model 2 (when $1/\mu = 10$ hrs. and k = 1).

We conclude from Figs. 5.6, 5.7, and 5.8 that the improvement by
introducing a standby unit to the two-unit multi system, is evident
as far as the availability and the MTBF are concerned, but not so evident as far as the computation availability is concerned when the mean
repair time is relatively small. That is, we can expect the improvements of the availability and the MTBF by introducing a standby unit
to the two-unit multi system (i.e., the three-unit hybrid redundant
system), but not expect that of the computation availability when the
mean repair time is relatively small.

We next consider the effect of the shape parameter k since var-
ying the shape parameter k implies some interesting repair time distributions shown in Fig. 5.5. We show in Fig. 5.9 the dependence of
the mean repair time $1/\mu$ on the unavailability for the two-unit multi
system, where k = 1, 2, 3, 5, and 10. We see from Fig. 5.9 that the
effect of the shape parameter k is not so evident, in particular,
when the mean repair time is relatively small. Fig. 5.10 shows the
dependence of the mean repair time $1/\mu$ on the unavailability for the
three-unit hybrid redundant system, where k = 1, 2, 3, 5, and 10.
Comparing Fig. 5.9 with Fig. 5.10, we see that the effect of the shape

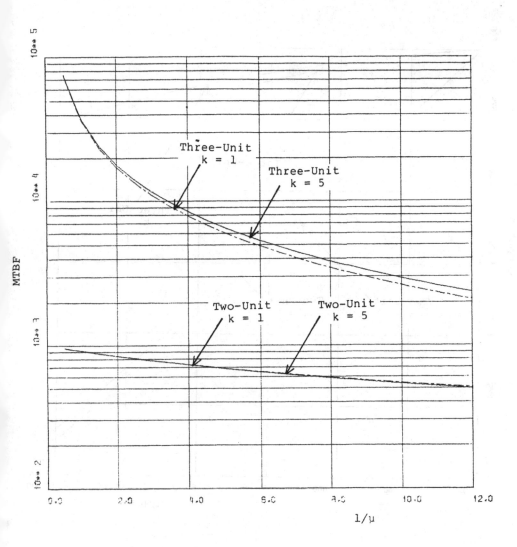

<u>Fig. 5.7.</u> The dependence of the mean repair time $1/\mu$ on the MTBF
for each system, where $k = 1, 5$; $1/\lambda_1 = 150$ hrs., $1/\lambda_{12} = 1,000$ hrs.,
and $1/\lambda_2 = 250$ hrs.

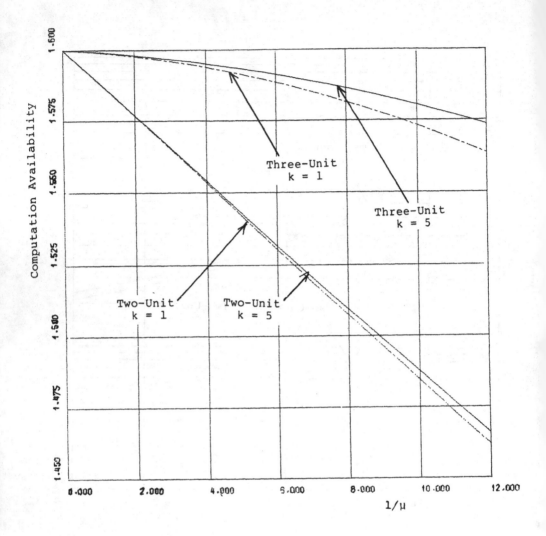

Fig. 5.8. The dependence of the mean repair time 1/μ on the computation   availability for each system, where k = 1, 5; 1/λ₁ = 150 hrs.,
1/λ₁₂ = 1,000 hrs., and 1/λ₂ = 250 hrs.

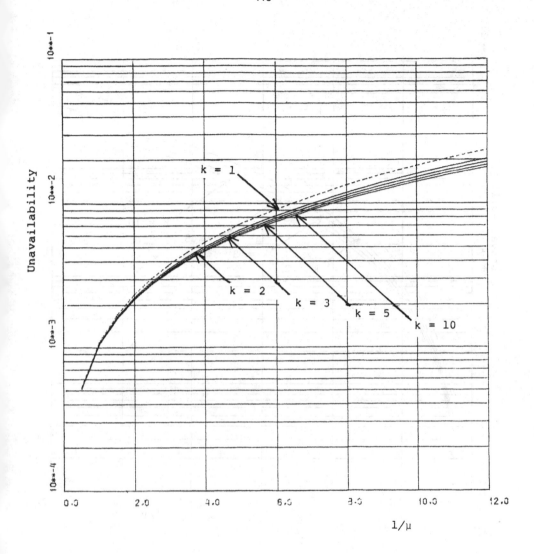

Fig. 5.9. The dependence of the mean repair time $1/\mu$ on the un-availability for the two-unit multi system, where $k = 1, 2, 3, 5, 10$; $1/\lambda_1 = 150$ hrs., and $1/\lambda_{12} = 1,000$ hrs.

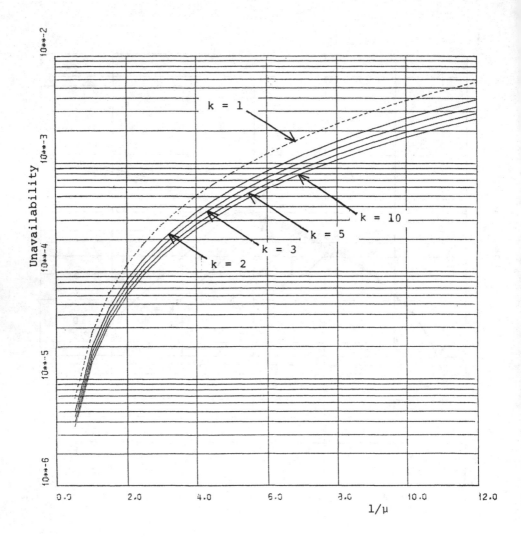

<u>Fig. 5.10.</u> The dependence of the mean repair time $1/\mu$ on the unavailability for the three-unit hybrid redundant system, where $k = 1, 2, 3, 5, 10$; $1/\lambda_1 = 150$ hrs., $1/\lambda_{12} = 1,000$ hrs., and $1/\lambda_2 = 250$ hrs.

parameter k is more evident as far as the three-unit hybrid redundant
system is concerned. Fig. 5.11 shows the dependence of the mean repair
time $1/\mu$ on the MTBF for the three-unit hybrid redundant system. We
see from Fig. 5.11 that the effect of the shape parameter k is not
so evident compared with that of the unavailability in Fig. 5.10.

We conclude from Figs. 5.9, 5.10, and 5.11 that the effect of the
shape parameter k in (5.62) is more evident for the three-unit hybrid
redundant system as far as the unavailability is concerned. That is,
we should specify the repair time distribution more precisely to analyze the computer systems. For instance, simple Markov models (see,
e.g., Beaudry (1978), Koren and Su (1979)) yield the distinction of
the real model if the non-exponential distribution is really included.
We recommend Markov Renewal Processes (MRP's) if available from this
reason.

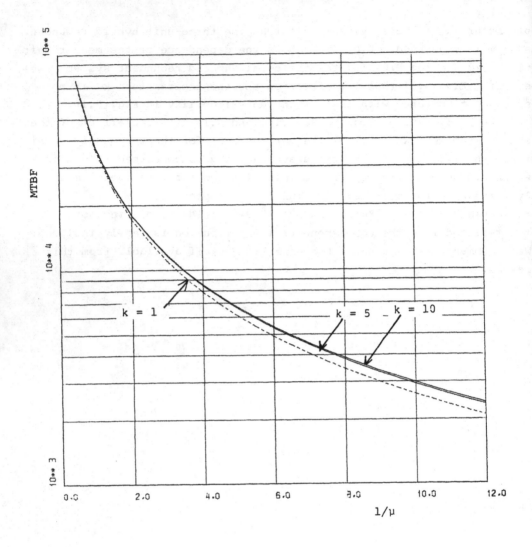

Fig. 5.11. The dependence of the mean repair time $1/\mu$ on the MTBF
for the three-unit hybrid redundant system, where k = 1, 5, 10; $1/\lambda_1$
= 150 hrs., $1/\lambda_{12}$ = 1,000 hrs., and $1/\lambda_2$ = 250 hrs.

MARKOV RENEWAL PROCESSES

A.1. Introduction

Throughout this book we apply Markov Renewal Processes (MRP's) as one of the mathematical tools of analysis. In the appendix we briefly sketch the preliminary properties of renewal processes and MRP's.

We discuss the failure rate of the lifetime distribution of an item, where an item is referred to as a part, an equipment, a material, and so on. The probability law of the lifetime of an item is given by a distribution with the non-negative random variable X:

$$F(t) = Pr\{X \leq t\}. \tag{A.1}$$

The probability density function is given by

$$f(t) = dF(t)/dt , \tag{A.2}$$

when it exists (we restrict ourselves to the continuous random variables throughout this book). Then, we define the __failure rate__

$$r(t) = f(t)/\overline{F}(t) , \tag{A.3}$$

when it exists and $\overline{F}(t) \equiv 1 - F(t) > 0$. We can explain the failure rate as follows: $r(t)dt$ is the probability that an item of age t will fail in the interval $(t, t+dt]$, given that the item survived at age t.

If we assume an exponential lifetime distribution

$$F(t) = 1 - e^{-\lambda t} \qquad (t \geq 0), \tag{A.4}$$

then

$$r(t) = \lambda e^{-\lambda t}/e^{-\lambda t} = \lambda , \tag{A.5}$$

which is constant. This property implies that a used exponential item
is essentially "as good as new." Only the exponential distribution
satisfies this property.

We discuss the exponential distribution from the viewpoint of the
conditional survival probability. Consider the conditional survival
probability

$$\Pr\{X > t + x \mid X > t\} = \Pr\{X > t + x\}/\Pr\{X > t\} \ , \tag{A.6}$$

which is the conditional probability that an item survives at time
$t + x$, given that it survived at time t. If we assume the exponential
distribution in (A.4), then

$$\Pr\{X > t + x \mid X > t\} = e^{-\lambda(t+x)}/e^{-\lambda t} = e^{-\lambda x} \ , \tag{A.7}$$

which is independent of the age history of the item. That is, the
exponential distribution is independent of the age history of the item
(i.e., how long the item is used since of the fresh item). We call
this property as the <u>memoryless property.</u> In general, the memoryless
property is given by the conditional survival probability

$$\Pr\{X > t + x \mid X > t\} = \Pr\{X > x\} \ , \tag{A.8}$$

or

$$\overline{F}(t + x) = \overline{F}(t)\overline{F}(x) \ , \tag{A.9}$$

by using the survival probability $\overline{F}(t) \equiv 1 - F(t)$. Let $\overline{F}(t)$ of a
nondegenerate non-negative random variable satisfy (A.9) for all $t \geq 0$,
$x \geq 0$. Then, we can show that F(t) is an exponential distribution
for some $\lambda > 0$ in (A.4). That is, the exponential distribution is
necessary and sufficient for the functional equation (A.9) (see Barlow
and Proschan (1975), Chapter 3).

If we assume a non-exponential distribution, the memoryless property is not satisfied any more. That is, we should know how long the
item is used since of the fresh item to analyze the stochastic behavior. For instance, we assume a gamma (or Erlang) distribution

$$F(t) = 1 - (1 + 2\lambda t)e^{-2\lambda t} \ , \tag{A.10}$$

where the mean is $1/\lambda$. Then, the failure rate is given by

$$r(t) = [dF(t)/dt]/\overline{F}(t) = 4\lambda^2 t/(1 + 2\lambda t) \; , \qquad\qquad (A.11)$$

which is increasing in t. That is, we never satisfy the memoryless property for this case.

A.2. Renewal Processes

A renewal process is defined as a sequence of independent, non-negative, and identically distributed random variables X_1, X_2, ..., which are not degenerate at time 0. Let us consider an example of a renewal process. For instance, if we consider a replacement problem of identical lamps during an infinite time operation, this replacement problem is described by a renewal process, where X_i is the lifetime of a lamp.

Let F(t) denote the inter-arrival distribution of the random variable X_i (i = 1, 2, ...). Define the random variable N(t) as the number of renewals (replacements) in (0, t]. Then

$$\Pr\{N(t) = n\} = \Pr\{X_1 + X_2 + \ldots + X_n \leq t \text{ and }$$
$$X_1 + X_2 + \ldots + X_{n+1} > t\}$$

$$= \Pr\{X_1 + X_2 + \ldots + X_n \leq t$$
$$- \Pr\{X_1 + X_2 + \ldots + X_{n+1} \leq t\}$$

$$= F^{(n)}(t) - F^{(n+1)}(t) \; , \qquad\qquad (A.12)$$

where $F^{(n)}(t)$ is the n-fold Stieltjes convolution of F(t) with itself, and $F^{(0)}(t)$ is a unit step function at t = 0. Let M(t) denote the renewal function which is the expected number of renewals in (0, t]. Then

$$M(t) = E[N(t)]$$

$$= \sum_{k=0}^{\infty} k \Pr\{N(t) = k\}$$

$$= \sum_{k=1}^{\infty} F^{(k)}(t) \; . \qquad\qquad (A.13)$$

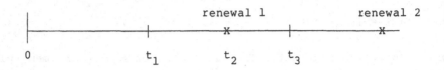

Fig. A.1.   A sample function of a renewal process.

We assume the non-exponential distribution F(t) in a renewal
process and consider a sample function shown in Fig. A.1.   The time
instant 0 is independent of the history since it is a starting point.
However, the time instant t_1 (or t_3) is not independent of the
history, but depends on the time duration t_1 (or $t_3 - t_2$) since
the non-exponential distribution has not the memoryless property.   The
time instant t_2 is independent of the history since it restarts as
the random variable X_2.   From Fig. A.1, we define that such the time
instants 0 and t_2 are <u>regeneration points</u> and such the time instants
t_1 and t_3 are <u>non-regeneration points</u>.   Renewal processes are developed on the basis of the regeneration points (or the regenerative
phenomena).

If we assume the exponential distribution in (A.4) in a renewal
process, then we can show that any time instant is a regeneration
point.   That is, we can specify at any time instant as a starting
point and obtain the corresponding results without any difficulty (recall the memoryless property of the exponential distribution).   In
general, a renewal process with the exponential inter-arrival distributions is called a Poisson process (see Ross (1970)).

A.3.   Markov Renewal Processes

We are interested in only the number of renewals in a renewal process.   That is, a renewal process is a one-state process which revisits
(renews) infinitely often during an infinite time duration.

An MRP is a stochastic process in which some different states are
introduced, the transition probabilities and the inter-arrival distributions from one state to another are specified.   We shall define an
MRP and briefly give some interesting results.   We restrict ourselves

to an MRP with finitely many states since the applications in reliability theory are mainly described by an MRP with finitely many states.

An MRP with finitely many states is defined as follows: Assume a finite number of states $i = 0, 1, 2, \ldots, N$. Define the transition probability

$Q_{ij}(t)$ = Pr{after making a transition into state i, the process
next makes a transition into state j, in an amount of
time less than or equal to t},

for any i and j, where

$$Q_{ij}(0) = 0 \qquad\qquad (i, j = 0, 1, \ldots, N), \qquad (A.14)$$

$$\sum_{j=0}^{N} Q_{ij}(\infty) = 1 \qquad\qquad (i = 0, 1, \ldots, N). \qquad (A.15)$$

We must define that the time instant i $(i = 0, 1, 2, \ldots, N)$, at which the process just makes a transition into state i, is a regeneration point. We define the unconditional sojourn distribution in state i

$$H_i(t) = \sum_{j=0}^{N} Q_{ij}(t) \qquad\qquad (i = 0, 1, 2, \ldots, N), \qquad (A.16)$$

not specifying any next visiting state. We define the random variable $X(t)$, where $X(t) = i$ denotes that the process is in state i at time t. We also define the random variable $N_i(t)$, where $N_i(t) = k$ denotes that the number of visit to state i is k in (0, t]. The <u>Markov renewal process</u> concerns with the random variables $N_i(t)$ $(i = 0, 1, \ldots, N)$. On the other hand, the <u>semi-Markov process</u> concerns with the random variable $X(t)$. We understand that both the MRP and the semi-Markov process are essentially the same stochastic processes. We just call the MRP's throughout this book.

Define the following quantities:

$$P_{ij}(t) = \Pr\{X(t) = j \mid X(0) = i\}, \qquad (A.17)$$

$$G_{ij}(t) = \Pr\{N_j(t) > 0 \mid X(0) = i\}, \qquad (A.18)$$

$$M_{ij}(t) = E[N_j(t) \mid X(0) = i], \qquad (A.19)$$

for i and j $(i, j = 0, 1, 2, \ldots, N)$. We note that $P_{ij}(t)$ denotes the probability that the process is in state j at time t, given that it was in state i at time 0, $G_{ij}(t)$ the first-passage distribution from state i to state j in $(0, t]$, and $M_{ij}(t)$ the generalized renewal function in state j (i.e., the mean number of visit to state j in $(0, t]$), given that the process was in state i at time 0. Recall the Stieltjes convolution defined in (1.9). Applying the renewal-theoretic arguments, we have

$$P_{ii}(t) = 1 - H_i(t) + \sum_{k=0}^{N} Q_{ik}(t)*P_{ki}(t) , \qquad (A.20)$$

$$P_{ij}(t) = \sum_{k=0}^{N} Q_{ik}(t)*P_{kj}(t) \qquad (i \neq j) , \qquad (A.21)$$

$$G_{ij}(t) = Q_{ij}(t) + \sum_{\substack{k=0 \\ k \neq j}}^{N} Q_{ik}(t)*G_{kj}(t) , \qquad (A.22)$$

$$M_{ij}(t) = G_{ij}(t) + G_{ij}(t)*M_{jj}(t) , \qquad (A.23)$$

for i and j $(i, j = 0, 1, 2, ..., N)$.

Let $q_{ij}(s)$, $h_i(s)$, $p_{ij}(s)$, and $m_{ij}(s)$ denote the Laplace-Stieltjes (LS) transforms of $Q_{ij}(t)$, $H_i(t)$, $P_{ij}(t)$, $G_{ij}(t)$, and $M_{ij}(t)$, respectively. Let $\underline{q}(s)$ and $\underline{m}(s)$ denote the matrices composed of $q_{ij}(s)$ and $m_{ij}(s)$, respectively. Then we take the LS transforms (A.21), (A.22), and (A.23) and solve them:

$$\underline{m}(s) = [\underline{I} - \underline{q}(s)]^{-1}\underline{q}(s) = [\underline{I} - \underline{q}(s)]^{-1} - \underline{I} , \qquad (A.24)$$

$$g_{ij}(s) = m_{ij}(s)/[1 + m_{jj}(s)] , \qquad (A.25)$$

$$p_{jj}(s) = [1 - h_j(s)]/[1 - g_{jj}(s)] , \qquad (A.26)$$

$$p_{ij}(s) = p_{jj}(s)g_{ij}(s) \qquad (i \neq j) , \qquad (A.27)$$

for i and j $(i, j = 0, 1, 2, ..., N)$, where $\underline{I}$ is the identity matrix. Equations (A.24) - (A.27) tell us that $\underline{q}(s) = [q_{ij}(s)]$ implies the LS transforms $m_{ij}(s)$, $g_{ij}(s)$, and $p_{ij}(s)$. However, it is generally difficult to invert the LS transforms analytically except the simplest cases. We should apply the numerical inversion (see Bellman et al. (1966)).

It is very difficult to discuss the transient behavior analytical-

ly since all the results in (A.24) - (A.27) are given by the LS transforms. However, it might be quite easy to discuss the limiting behavior analytically. We first introduce the notion of an embedded Markov
Chain (MC). That is, an embedded MC of an MRP is an MC in which any
one-step transition duration from one state to another is regarded as
a unit of time. The transition probability matrix Q of the embedded
MC is derived by the limiting operation:

$$Q = [q_{ij}] , \tag{A.28}$$

which we call as the limiting transition probability matrix since each
element is the limiting transition probability

$$q_{ij} = \lim_{s \to 0} q_{ij}(s) = \lim_{t \to \infty} Q_{ij}(t) . \tag{A.29}$$

We assume that the embedded MC of the MRP is positive recurrent
(i.e., all the states communicate). Then we have the positive stationary distribution $\pi = [\pi_0 , \pi_1 , \ldots, \pi_N]$ as a unique solution to
equations:

$$\pi = \pi \cdot Q \qquad \text{and} \qquad \sum_{i=0}^{N} \pi_i = 1 \tag{A.30}$$

(see Ross (1970)). Barlow and Proschan (1965) showed the mean first
passage ℓ_{ij} for the MRP as follows:

$$\ell_{ij} = \sum_{\substack{k=0 \\ k \neq j}}^{N} q_{ik} \ell_{kj} + \mu_i \qquad (i, j = 0, 1, \ldots, N), \tag{A.31}$$

where

$$\mu_i = \int_0^\infty t \, dH_i(t) \qquad (i = 0, 1, \ldots, N) \tag{A.32}$$

is the unconditional mean of the distribution $H_i(t)$. By using the
stationary distribution π and the matrix manipulations, we have

$$\ell_{ii} = \sum_{k=0}^{N} \pi_k \mu_k / \pi_i \qquad (i = 0, 1, \ldots, N). \tag{A.33}$$

Generalizing the renewal theorem (see Ross (1970)), we can show

$$M_j \equiv \lim_{t \to \infty} M_{ij}(t)/t = 1/\ell_{jj} \qquad (i, j = 0, 1, \ldots, N). \tag{A.34}$$

Applying the above results to (A.26) and (A.27), we have

$$P_j \equiv \lim_{t \to \infty} P_{ij}(t) = \mu_j/\ell_{jj} = \pi_j \mu_j / \sum_{k=0}^{N} \pi_k \mu_k$$

$$(i, j = 0, 1, \ldots, N). \qquad (A.35)$$

Note that M_j and P_j are independent of a starting state i. The interesting results (A.33), (A.34), and (A.35) are based on the assumption that all the states of the embedded MC (or the MRP) communicate.

We have given the brief results of the MRP's. The detailed discussions were given by Pyke (1961a, 1961b), Barlow and Proschan (1965), Ross (1970), and Cinlar (1975). The unique modification of the regeneration point techniques of MRP's was developed by Nakagawa and Osaki (1974, 1976). Throughout this book we apply the unique modification of MRP's to the models of computer architectures to analyze the MRP's with some non-regeneration points.

REFERENCES

Some references listed below are not cited in the text. However, we include these references since they are closely related to the topics in this book. All references listed below are in alphabetical order.

Y. Abe (1977), "A Japanese On-Line Banking System," Datamation, vol. 23, pp. 89-97.

Y. Abe, Y. Ueno, A. Honma, E. Kato, Y. Nose, Y. Yasufuku and M. Atarashi (1977), "The Dai-Ichi Kangyo Bank, LTD - HOPS: Development and System Configuration," (in Japanese) FUJITSU, vol. 28, pp. 856-892.

T. Anderson and B. Randell (Ed.) (1979), Computing Systems Reliability, Cambridge University Press, Cambridge.

T.F. Arnold (1973), "The Concept of Coverage and Its Effect on the Reliability Model of a Repairable System," IEEE Trans. Comput., vol. C-22, pp. 251-254.

A. Avizienis (1976), "Fault-Tolerant Systems," IEEE Trans. Comput., vol. C-25, pp. 1304-1312.

A. Avizienis, G.C. Gilley, F.P. Mathur, D.A. Rennels, J.A. Rohr and D.K. Rubin (1971), "The STAR (Self-Testing And Repairing) Computer: An Investigation of the Theory and Practice of Fault-Tolerant Computer Design," IEEE Trans. Comput., vol. C-20, pp. 1312-1321.

R.E. Barlow and F. Proschan (1965), Mathematical Theory of Reliability, Wiley, New York.

R.E. Barlow and F. Proschan (1975), Statistical Theory of Reliability and Life Testing - Probability Models, Holt, Rinehart and Winston, New York.

M.D. Beaudry (1978), "Performance-Related Reliability Measures for Computing Systems," IEEE Trans. Comput., vol. C-27, pp. 540-547.

R. Bellman, R.E. Kalaba and J. Lockett (1966), Numerical Inversion of the Laplace Transform, American Elsevier, New York.

B.R. Borgerson and R.F. Freitas (1975), "A Reliability Model for Gracefully Degrading and Standby-Sparing Systems," IEEE Trans. Comput., vol. C-24, pp. 517-525.

W.G. Bouricius, W.C. Carter, D.C. Jessep, P.R. Schneider and A.B.
Wadia (1971), "Reliability Modeling for Fault-Tolerant Computers,"
IEEE Trans. Comput., vol. C-20, pp. 1306-1311.

W.G. Bouricius, W.C. Carter and P.R. Schneider (1969), "Reliability
Modeling Techniques for Self-Repairing Computer Systems," in Proc.
12th ACM Nat. Conf., pp. 295-309.

W.C. Carter and W.G. Bouricius (1971), "A Survey of Fault-Tolerant
Computer Architecture and Its Evaluation," Computer, vol. 4, pp.
9-16.

G.A. Champine (1978), Computer Technology Impact on Management, North
-Holland Publishing Company, Amsterdam.

T.C.K. Chou and J.A. Abraham (1980), "Performance/Availability Model
of Shared Resource Multiprocessors," IEEE Trans. Reliab., vol.
R-29, to appear.

D.K. Chow (1975), "Availability of Some Repairable Computer Systems,"
IEEE Trans. Reliab., vol. R-24, pp. 64-66.

E. Cinlar (1975), Introduction to Stochastic Processes, Prentice-Hall,
Englewood Cliffs, New Jersey,

A.E. Cooper and W.T. Chow (1976), "Development of On-Board Computer
Systems," IBM J. Res. Develop., vol 20, pp. 5-19.

A. Costes, C. Landrault and J.C. Laprie (1978), "Reliability and Availability Models for Maintained Systems Featuring Hardware Failures
and Design Faults," IEEE Trans. Comput., vol. C-27, pp. 548-560.

A.L. Hopkins, Jr. and T.B. Smith (1975), "The Architectural Elements
of a Symmetric Fault-Tolerant Multiprocessor," IEEE Trans. Comput.,
vol. C-24, pp. 498-505.

M. Kajiyama and S. Osaki (1979), "Performance-Related Analyses for
Computer Systems with High Reliability," (in Japanese) Trans. IECE
Japan, vol. J62-D, pp. 742-749.

M. Kinugasa and S. Osaki (1979), "Analysis of Highly Reliable Redundant
Computer Systems Taking Account of Performance," (in Japanese)
IECE Technical Reports on Reliability, R79-29, pp. 23-29.

M. Kinugasa and S. Osaki (1980), "Reliability Analysis of a Three-Unit
Standby Redundant System," (in Japanese) Abstracts presented in the Spring
Meeting of Operations Res. Soc. Japan, pp. 144-145.

I. Koren and S.Y.H. Su (1979), "Reliability Analysis of N-Modular Redundant Systems with Intermittent and Permanent Faults," IEEE
Trans. Comput., vol. C-28, pp. 514-520.

J.C. Laprie (1976), "On Reliability Prediction of Repairable Redundant
Digital Structures," IEEE Trans. Reliab., vol. R-25, pp. 275-277.

J. Losq (1976), "A Highly Efficient Redundancy Scheme: Self-Purging Redundancy," IEEE Trans. Comput., vol. C-25, pp. 569-578.

F.P. Mathur and A. Avizienis (1970), "Reliability Analysis and Architecture of a Highly Redundant Digital System: Generalized Triple Modular Redundancy with Self-Repair," in Proc. 1970 SJCC, AFIPS Conf. Proc., vol. 36, pp. 375-383.

F.P. Mathur and P.T. de Souza (1975), "Reliability Modeling and Analysis of Generalized Modular Redundant Systems," IEEE Trans. Reliab., vol. R-24, pp. 296-299.

T. Nakagawa and S. Osaki (1974), "Stochastic Behaviour of a Two-Unit Standby Redundant System," INFOR, vol. 12, pp. 66-70.

T. Nakagawa and S. Osaki (1976), "Markov Renewal Processes with Some Non-Regeneration Points and Their Applications to Reliability Theory," Microelectron. Reliab., vol. 15, pp. 633-636.

S. Osaki (1970), "System Reliability Analysis by Markov Renewal Processes," J. Operations Res. Soc. Japan, vol. 12, pp. 127-188.

S. Osaki (1974), "Signal-Flow Graphs in Reliability Theory," Microelectron. Reliab., vol. 13, pp. 539-541.

S. Osaki and T. Nakagawa (1976), "Bibliography for Reliability and Availability for Stochastic Systems," IEEE Trans. Reliab., vol. R-25, pp. 284-287.

S. Osaki and T. Nishio (1979), "Availability Evaluation of Redundant Computer Systems," Comput. Operations Res., vol. 6, pp. 87-97.

R. Pyke (1961a), "Markov Renewal Processes: Definitions and Preliminary Properties," Ann. Math. Statist., vol. 32, pp. 1231-1242.

R. Pyke (1961b), "Markov Renewal Processes with Finitely Many States," Ann. Math. Statist., vol. 32, pp. 1243-1259.

B. Randell (1975), "System Structure for Software Fault-Tolerance," IEEE Trans. Software Eng., vol. SE-1, pp. 220-232.

S.M. Ross (1970), Applied Probability Models with Optimization Applications, Holden-Day, San Francisco.

R.A. Short (1968), "The Attainment of Reliable Digital Systems Through the Use of Redundancy - A Survey," IEEE Comput. Group News, vol. 2, pp. 2-17.

Y. Suzuki, T. Nakagawa and Y. Sawa (1977), "Reliability Analysis of Computer Systems with High Reliability," (in Japanese) Trans. IECE Japan, vol. J60-D, pp. 1047-1052.

J. von Neumann (1956), "Probabilistic Logics and the Synthesis of Reliable Organizations from Unreliable Components," in Autamata Studies, C.E. Shannon and J. McCarthy (Ed.), Princeton University Press, Princeton, New Jersey.

This series reports new developments in computer science research and teaching – quickly, informally and at a high level. The type of material considered for publication includes:

1. Preliminary drafts of original papers and monographs
2. Lectures on a new field or presentations of a new angle in a classical field
3. Seminar work-outs
4. Reports of meetings, provided they are
   a) of exceptional interest and
   b) devoted to a single topic.

Texts which are out of print but still in demand may also be considered if they fall within these categories.

The timeliness of a manuscript is more important than its form, which may be unfinished or tentative. Thus, in some instances, proofs may be merely outlined and results presented which have been or will later be published elsewhere. If possible, a subject index should be included. Publication of Lecture Notes is intended as a service to the international computer science community, in that a commercial publisher, Springer-Verlag, can offer a wide distribution of documents which would otherwise have a restricted readership. Once published and copyrighted, they can be documented in the scientific literature.

Manuscripts

Manuscripts should be no less than 100 and preferably no more than 500 pages in length.

They are reproduced by a photographic process and therefore must be typed with extreme care. Symbols not on the typewriter should be inserted by hand in indelible black ink. Corrections to the typescript should be made by pasting in the new text or painting out errors with white correction fluid. Authors receive 75 free copies and are free to use the material in other publications. The typescript is reduced slightly in size during reproduction; best results will not be obtained unless the text on any one page is kept within the overall limit of 18 x 26.5 cm (7 x 10½ inches). On request, the publisher will supply special paper with the typing area outlined.

Manuscripts should be sent to Prof. G. Goos, Institut für Informatik, Universität Karlsruhe, Zirkel 2, 7500 Karlsruhe/Germany, Prof. J. Hartmanis, Cornell University, Dept. of Computer-Science, Ithaca, NY/USA 14850, or directly to Springer-Verlag Heidelberg.

Springer-Verlag, Heidelberger Platz 3, D-1000 Berlin 33
Springer-Verlag, Neuenheimer Landstraße 28–30, D-6900 Heidelberg 1
Springer-Verlag, 175 Fifth Avenue, New York, NY 10010/USA

ISBN 3-540-10274-4
ISBN 0-387-10274-4